FAITHFUL SERVANTS

PASTORS
OF
ST. JOHN THE BAPTIST CATHOLIC CHURCH
PRINCETON, WISCONSIN

by

Roger F. Krentz, Ph.D.

ISBN: 978-1-257-98420-6

Copyright © 2011 Roger F. Krentz, Ph.D.

All Rights Reserved

No part of this publication may be reproduced,
Stored in a retrieval system or transmitted
In any form or by any means without prior
written permission from the author.

*Let Thy priests, O Lord, be clothed with justice,
and let Thy saints rejoice;
for Thy servant David's sake,
turn not away the face of Thy anointed.*
                                    Ps 131. 9-10

O ye priests of the Lord, bless the Lord:
O ye servants of the Lord, sing a hymn unto God.
Dan. 3. 84-85

Dedication

To the priest who baptized me,
Rev. Thomas Jankowski
and
to the priest who heard my first confession
and
from whom I received my First Holy Communion,
Rev. Francis S. Karwata

The Lord hath sworn, and He will not repent:
Thou art a priest for ever according to the order of Melchiesedeck
Ps. 100.4

TABLE OF CONTENTS

Introduction ….. 9

Pastors ….. 15
   Diocese of Green Bay (1868-1905) ….. 17
   Archdiocese of Milwaukee (1905-1945) ….. 47
   Diocese of Madison (1945-present) ….. 61

Conclusion ….. 73

Appendix A Pastors ….. 77

Appendix B Bishops ….. 79

Appendix C Other Parishes ….. 80

Appendix D Other Priests ….. 84

Bibliography ….. 85

Acknowledgements ….. 88

Good and faithful servant, enter thou into the joy of the Lord.
Matt. 25. 21

INTRODUCTION

His Holiness, Pope Benedict XVI declared the year June 2009 to June 2010 to be the Year of the Priest. On the Feast of the Sacred heart of Jesus, 11 June 2010, His Holiness, Pope Benedict XVI closed the Year of the Priest. In his homily he said, "The priest is not a mere officeholder, like those which every society needs in order to carry out certain functions.

"Instead, he does something which no human being can do of his own power: in Christ's name he speaks the words which absolve us of our sins and in this way he changes, starting with God, our entire life.

"Over the offerings of bread and wine he speaks Christ's words of thanksgiving, which are words of transubstantiation—words which make Christ himself present, the Risen One, his Body and Blood—words which thus transform the elements of the world, which open the world to God and unite it to him.

"The priesthood, then, is not simply 'office' but sacrament: God makes use of us poor men in order to be, through us, present to all men and women, and to act on their behalf.

"The audacity of God who entrusts himself to human beings—who, conscious of our weaknesses, nonetheless considers men capable of acting and being present in his stead—this audacity of God is the true grandeur concealed in the word 'priesthood'."

What more appropriate time to pay tribute to the priests who served the Catholics of our home parish, St. John the Baptist Catholic Church, Princeton, Wisconsin.

We have all heard the story of Father Jacques Marquette's expedition down the Fox River in 1673, the blessing of the spring at St. Marie and the erection of a cross at the spring. This may have been the first introduction of Catholicism to the Princeton area.

Closely related to Father Marquette's spring and the cross is the church of St. Marie in the former village of St. Marie. This would be the second major recorded appearance of Catholicism in the Princeton, WI area. It is known that Reverend Anthony Godfert (Godfrey) built a small brick chapel dedicated to St. Mary of the Spring in 1854-55. This chapel commemorated the legend that Father Jacques Marquette and Joliet when traveling the Fox River over 300 years ago, stopped near this village of St. Marie. It commemorated Father Marquette blessing a spring at this place and erecting a cross.

Father Godfert (Godfrey) was the first missionary priest to celebrate Holy Mass for the Catholics in Montello, WI in the 1850s. There he constructed a small log church about a mile from the old Church of St. John the Baptist in Montello. Reverend Godfert (Godfrey) ministered to the Catholics of St. Stephen's, Stevens Point, and St. Joseph's Berlin among others.

The first known Catholic church on the west side of the Fox River in the immediate Princeton area in the 1850s was located on the Fred Laboyewski farm (in 1987 on the Norman Rohde farm on Eagle Lane). To my knowledge no one has ever definitively found the exact location. Like most of the mission churches in Wisconsin during this period in our history, it would have been either a very simple frame structure or a log structure. From the research done, the simple frame churches were about 16 feet by 16 feet. We don't know the size of the first church at Princeton, but undoubtedly it was very small. These mission churches were used infrequently by missionary priests who were making a circuit ministering to the Catholic in the region. Generally the missionary priest would lodge with the nearest Catholic family in the vicinity.

Rev. Bolek maintains Rev. L. Sylvester Szczepankiewicz was the first priest/pastor of St. John the Baptist, Princeton from 1867-1868 (Bolek, 1943, p. 446). He could very well be correct. This is one of only two references to this priest that could be found. However, I would maintain that Father Anthony Godfert (Godfrey) was instrumental in the erection of this first church on the west side of the Fox River in Princeton, WI. He did establish the church at Montello and the one at St. Marie. Besides there were Polish and other Catholics living in the Princeton area since the 1850s.

As you may know, Poland was partitioned three times among Russia, Prussia and Austria beginning in 1772 and finalized by 1792. Thus Poland was wiped from the face of the earth until after World War I. This had numerous implications for the Poles living within the former geographic boundaries of Poland and for those who emigrated elsewhere. They totally lost their national identity and were incorporated into the partitioning countries. They were generally considered "second class" citizens, a conquered people; couldn't use their native language in public transactions, school, etc.; were persecuted for their religious beliefs; monasteries and convents were suppressed. Numerous Poles opted to leave their homeland and emigrate to other parts of Europe and the world. Today, we find civil records of our Polish ancestors that indicate they were German, Russian or Austrian when in fact, they were really Polish. Most of the Poles who came to settle in the Princeton, Green Lake County area were from the Prussian partition of Poland.

In 1870 Reverend Bonaventura Buczyński was assigned by Bishop John Martin Henni, Bishop of Milwaukee, to establish the St. Stanislaus Kostka Parish in Princeton, WI on the east side of the Fox River. This was a very short lived parish—only until 1872.

"A second Catholic Church is to be built this season. The one on the east side of the river is being built by the Polish Catholics, and August Swanke, German, has the contract for building one of the same size on the west side of the river. It would be much better if both factions could have united and put up one large church. Each one is to be 30 by 40 feet, on the ground with height of room 16 feet. The east side church will be of stone, the west side one of wood." (Princeton Republic vol. V, no. 15). The Archdiocese of Milwaukee has lost much information on the foundations of early parishes under its jurisdiction. Therefore, it cannot be determined the priest who organized this parish and erected the church. We can be sure Bishop Henni would have given permission for the organization of a parish if there were between 20 and 30 families requesting the foundation with the ability to support the church.

In the 28 October 1871 issue of the Princeton Republic vol. V, no. 41, it says, "The Polish Catholic Church on the west side has just been completed at an expense of about $3,000. The church being somewhat in debt, hereby appeals to all to assist in paying of the same—Andros Barthol—Antone Domask." Unfortunately, we don't know who the priest was that was instrumental in erecting this wooden church.

"The most pervasive influence on the life of Polish immigrants in America during the period of mass migration was religion. In partitioned Poland, the Church transcended the boundaries of the three regions, providing both a unifying factor and a haven for the expression of Polish nationalism. In America, immigrants unfamiliar with the language or culture of their new environment relied on the familiarity of their deeply held religious convention and institutions as a stabilizing element in their otherwise uncertain lives. In addition, in America, as in Poland, the local parish was central to the daily secular life of Poles, serving as a source of personal recognition and social interaction. The local parish priest functioned as a spiritual father, temporal leader, priest, teacher, legal advisor, business advisor, and representative to the outside world of business, government, and society." (Pula 1995 p. 38).

Most, if not all, of the Polish parishes in Wisconsin were started with lay initiatives. The people of an area would petition the local bishop for the establishment of a parish church and request the assignment of a Polish priest. "The Polish parish in American was a reflection of both Polish religious conviction and pride in collective accomplishment. The very extravagance of the buildings and furnishings of Polish American churches, standing as it did in sharp contrast to their Spartan life, was a measure of the immigrants' joint success." (Pula 1995 p. 39). Over and over again across Wisconsin, we can find Polish immigrants not only giving the little money they had, but also, their time and energy in building the local parish church. "These congregations, however, were more than interconnected islands of Polishness in the New World; they were also the most tangible sign of Polish presence with the institutional Church." (Kuzniewski, 1973 p. 1).

Roman Catholicism for the Poles was not just a Sunday religion. Much of their lives were regulated by religious feast days, saints' days and the religious Catholic calendar year.

Dedicating this Polish church in Princeton to St. John the Baptist is not unusual. Some of the early Polish immigrants to Princeton came from St. John the Baptist Catholic Church, Ludomy, County of Oborniki, Poznań, Poland. The parish of St. John the Baptist in Ludomy dates from 1459 (Sulimierski 1902 v.5, p. 469-70) and is still active today. Numerous parishes across Poland are dedicated to St. John the Baptist. The Poles have long held for many centuries St. John the Baptist as the bringer of rain for crops. It is natural, therefore, for these first parishioners, who were farmers, to name their church in honor of St. John the Baptist.

The contractor for the erection of the St. John the Baptist Catholic Church on the west side of the Fox River was August Swanke. He came to Princeton, Wisconsin in 1856, married Minnie Dundee in 1857, fathered eight children. In 1866 he erected a large stone building that was used as a blacksmith shop and in 1873 erected another large stone building where he constructed carriages. He was a public servant, serving as Chairman of the

Board of Supervisors, President of the Town Board among others. (Portrait and Biographical Album of Green Lake.... 1890, p. 591-2).

By looking at pictures of the St. John the Baptist Catholic Church built in 1871, we are struck by the beauty and simplicity of the structure. The style is very much in the Greek Revival fashion, often used in public buildings of this period. You see the broad corner pilasters and architrave, characteristic of this type of architecture in the United States. There were three arched windows on each side and double doors in the front with an arched windor over it. It may have had a stove for heat in the winter and a very simple chandelier to provide some lighting. Sometimes in churches like this one, there may have been a small room for a sacristy off the sanctuary or behind it. This room could double as a place for the priest to live while there. The edifice had a small, open belfry over the front doorway surmounted by a cross.

The interior would have been very plain and simple. The windows may have been clear or frosted glass. The main altar would have been extremely simple with a small tabernacle in the center of the reredos and a raised step on each side for candles. Over the tabernacle would have been the crucifix. There may have been a statue or picture on the wall over the main altar. There would have been a Communion rail. There would have been a picture or statue of the Blessed Virgin May, perhaps Our Lady of Częstchowa. The pews would have been simple benches, with or without backs. This church would remain without a resident pastor until February 1875.

At the time when most of the Poles settled in the Princeton area of Green Lake County, Wisconsin, the United States of America was a missionary country. This missionary status remained until November 1908. Recently, the United States is once again considered to be a missionary country. All the pastors/priests who ministered at St. John the Baptist Catholic Church, Princeton were missionaries—from Rev. Joseph Szpecht (the first resident pastor) to Rev. Sigmund Wozńy. Rev. Joseph C. Knitter was the first pastor who was not a missionary in a missionary country.

The hardships faced by the early missionary priests is difficult to comprehend by the present day reader. Various accounts have been written either in autobiographical fashion (Servant of God Samuel Mazzuchelli's memoirs) or in biographical accounts (i.e. Hoffman, 1837 [Anthony Godfert] p. 169; Lorimer, 2009, [Casper Rehrl] first two chapters). Keep in mind, missionary priests served numerous churches and chapels in a given area. Sometimes, these missionary priests crossed paths and served each other's churches in the same area. During their tenure in Wisconsin some missionary priests may have had a home base church and a rectory of sorts. When they were on their missionary treks which were generally on foot, they relied on the kindness of the local Catholics for meals and a place to sleep.

Courtesy of Krentz Collection

PASTORS

We are looking at the priests who served as resident pastors of St. John the Baptist Catholic Church, Princeton. St. John's since its foundation in 1870, it has been under three diocesan jurisdictions—Green Bay, Milwaukee, and Madison. The enumerating of the Pastors will be divided by diocesan jurisdiction.

As you will see, some of the priests at St. John's served for a very limited time in Princeton. I am not sure the reason for this and none of the diocesan authorities I consulted could explain it either. One theory was that as missionaries in a mission country/state, priests were given more latitude by their Bishop in moving from parish to parish. However, that seems odd to me, because there generally was another priest assigned (or arriving) soon after the departure of a pastor. Someone must have known about departures and arrivals. It must have been disconcerting for the parishioners never knowing who will be their priest the next Sunday. The short tenure at parishes was not only here in Princeton, but can be found in almost all of the Polish parishes (at least) across the state.

Little is known about some of the priests who served at St. John's, especially the early pastors. Some of these early pastors eventually left the Wisconsin dioceses and labored in other states, returned to Europe or some other mission field. Diocesan records and information is lacking as to their other pastoral work. We do know most, if not all, the early priests here served in other Polish parishes. Some of the priests founded several other parishes in Wisconsin. Others seemed to follow each other, some serving many of the same parishes consecutively or intermittently.

One thing is certain, all the priests serving at St. John the Baptist parish had to speak Polish in order to minister properly to the flock. Most, if not all, the priests from the partitioned Poland would have known Polish either as a first or second language. Besides, they would have known German, Russian or another language depending on where they lived. The same would be true for most of the St. John's Polish parishioners.

Pastors have great influence on the life of a parish either for good or bad. Pastors come and go, but the parishioners remain. If the pastor's leadership is positive the parish thrives and grows in conformity to Christ. If negative parishes become dysfunctional they are lead away from Christ by the hireling. Thankfully, for the most part the priests who shepherded St. John the Baptist congregation have been true shepherds of Christ's flock in Princeton.

ST. JOHN THE BAPTIST CATHOLIC CHURCH
PRINCETON, WISCONSIN
DIOCESE OF GREEN BAY
(1868-1905)

1. Rev. Joseph Szpecht   Feb. 1875-Sept 1875

Even though a church was built in Princeton in 1870, it wasn't until February 1875 that Bishop Henni would assign a priest as the first resident pastor of St. John the Baptist Catholic Church, Princeton. Thus, **Reverend Joseph Szpecht (Specht)** became the first of twenty-two priests to be resident pastors in Princeton. Unfortunately, nothing is known about Father Szpecht except that he remained at St. John's until September 1875. Rev. Szpecht formally dedicated this parish church on 17 April 1875 to St. John the Baptist. "St. John the Baptist Church was established as a mission in the Green Bay Diocese in 1875." (Krystofiak 1987, p.2).

2. Rev. Januarius Czarnowski   Sept 1875-July 1877

The second resident pastor of St. John the Baptist Catholic Church was **Rev. Januarius Czarnowski**, Missionary Apostolic, who became pastor in September 1875. He was incardinated into the Diocese of Green Bay in 1875, This was his first assignment in the United States and the Diocese of Green Bay. He was born 30 April 1845 in Strassburg, West Prussia and christened "Konstanty". He studied theology at the Franciscan monastery in Culm, West Prussia, Poland. It appears he entered the Franciscan Order at that time and thus, received the name of Januarius. (Rev. Kruszak referes to him as an ex-Franciscan on p. 78 of his 1908 history of Poles in American). Right Reverend Jeshke, Bishop of Culm, West Prussia ordained him to the priesthood on 21 September 1873. He served the first two years of his priesthood in his native land. Fr. Czarnowski emigrated to the United States of America in 1875. He served his Polish flock in Princeton until July 1877.

Father Januarius Czarnowski was assigned to St. Casimir Catholic Church, Hull (Kazimierz), Wisconsin in the Diocese of La Crosse in October 1878. While there he embellished the church by buying three altars for $1000.

While he was at St. Casimir, he ministered to the people at St. Peter's Catholic Church, Steven Point. He remained at St. Casimir's until May 1886. St. Casimir's was without a pastor for seven months once Rev. Czarnowski left.

Rev. Czarnowski was assigned to St. Stanislaus Kostka Catholic Church, Berlin, WI in the Diocese of Green Bay in May 1886. While in Berlin from 1892 onward, Rev. Czarnowski held the honorary office of diocesan consultant in the Diocese of Green Bay. Pope Pius IX conferred upon Rev. Czarnowski the honorary title of Missionary Apostolic for his missionary labors among the Polish Catholics in the United States. While at St. Stanislaus Kostka parish, Berlin, WI his housekeeper was Theresa Czajkowski.

Rev. Januarius Czarnowski died as pastor of St. Stanislaus Kostka Church, Berlin on 18 September 1898. He is buried in St. Stanislaus Kostka Catholic Cemetery, Berlin, WI next to the grave of the priest founder of St. Stanislaus Kostka Catholic Church, the Polish missionary priest, Rev. Bonaventura Buczyński.

Courtesy of RFK
Rev. Januarius Czarnowski's grave in St. Stanislaus Kostka's Catholic Cemetery, Berlin, WI

3. Rev. Adam Bukowski   July 1877-August 1877

The third pastor of St. John the Baptist Catholic Church, Princeton was **Rev. Adam (some places Adalbert, Wojciech) Bukowski,** born ca. 1847. Rev. Bukowski arrived in July 1877 and left in August 1877. After leaving Princeton, Rev. Bukowski was pastor at St. Peter's Catholic Church, Stevens Point for a short time, during which he ministered to the faithful at St. Joseph's in Poniatowski, WI. Rev. Adam Bukowski was a given the honorary title of Missionary Apostolic by Pope Pius IX for his missionary activities among the Polish Catholics in the United States. After his service in Stevens Point, nothing is known of his missionary activities.

4. Rev. John Ignatius Zawistowski   Sept 1877-Dec 1879

Next **Rev. John Ignatius Zawistowski (Zawitowski, Zavistowski)** became pastor in September 1877 of St. john the Baptist parish, Princeton, WI. Rev. Zawistowski was born 11 August 1822 in Płock, Poland. He entered the Discalced Carmelite Order and was ordained 19 December 1846 in Germany. He was a missionary in India for some time. He arrive in the United States in April 1857 where he ministered to the Catholics of many places including the Diocese of Brooklyn, NY. On 15 April 1864 a passport was issued to Rev. Zawistowski while he was in the State of New York, County of Erie, City of Buffalo to travel to Europe, particularly Austria to visit friends and family. At the time he was 42 years old, described as five feet, eight inches tall with grey eyes. He is listed in the 1860 U.S. census in Buffalo, NY. On 23 October 1863 Rev. Zawistowski became a naturalized citizen in Buffalo, NY (Naturalization Record 1863). His housekeeper at this time was Josephine Herbst from Bavaria. He was incardinated into the Diocese of Green Bay in 1869. By 1870 Rev. Zawistowski is already in Kewaunee County, Wisconsin. Josephine Herbst is still his housekeeper. He was "assigned to parishes in the diocese as follows: Two Rivers, St. Luke's, 1870; Algoma (then listed as St. Raphael's Ahnapee), 1873; Oshkosh, St. Mary's" (Long, 1983 p.425), 1874-77 before coming to Princeton. After December 1879 he is listed as a substitute pastor for Father Wałuń at St. Peter's, Steven Point for November and December 1881; pastor of St. Michael's, Beaver Dam, 1882-83. He was pastor of St. John Nepomuc (later called St. Anthony), Highland, WI in 1885. He could preach in Polish, Bohemian and German. However, in this German parish, he preached mostly in German. He is probably remembered by most people on account of the strange way in which he met his untimely death.

"Father John Zawistowski met his untimely death by a freak accident. He was summoned to a sick call to Mary Huza.. She was a girl about fourteen and was working at the Ferdinand Delkamp home. John Jansen was going to take him there. He had a fast, snappy team hitched to what was generally called a 'milk wagon.' There were two seats as wide as the box, one up front and one in the back. These seats were spring seats mounted on two iron hooks that hung over the top edge on each side of the wagon box. Father John mounted the milk wagon on the back seat, from the sidewalk just a little south of the church. When Mr. Jansen said 'Giddyapp' (some say he cracked the whip) the horses jerked the wagon forward so violently that Father John was thrown over backward onto the ground. He suffered a broken neck and died a few days later on May 14, 1889. He is the second priest to be buried in St. Anthony's cemetery." (The Centennial Story of St. Anthony's Parish, 1960, p. 31). His funeral was held on 19 May 1889 at St. John's, Highland. He was known as an eloquent preacher and was a popular priest. (Princeton Times Republic vol. XXIII 23 May 1889).

From "Catholic Church in Wisconsin" p. 1057
Reverend John Ignatius Zawistowski

Courtesy of RFK
(left) Front of Rev. Zawistowski's tombstone with Sacedotal symbols. The inscription could not be read without a rubbing. (right) the back of the tombstone in St. John Nepumuc/St. Anthony's cemetery, Highland, WI

5. Rev. Klemens Rogożiński   Dec 1879-June 1884

Reverend Klemens Ludwig Rogożiński (Rogodziński, Ragoziński) succeeded Rev. Zawistowski in December 1879 and served the parish until June 1884. On 21 November 1883, the feast of the Presentation of the Blessed Virgin Mary in the temple, under Rev. Rogożiński's pastorate, this mission of St. John the Baptist, Princeton was incorporated as a parish. Reverend Wacław Kruszka lists St. John the Baptist Parish as the ninth Polish parish in Wisconsin (Kruszka 1924, vol. 1. p. 696). Rev. Rogoziński can be credited with building the comfortable brick rectory in 1881 which still stands today. He was born in Sierpe, Kingdom of Poland on 24 August 1835. "He joined the Order of the Bernardine Fathers and was ordained in

Łowicz in 1861 at the time when the [January] uprising was being prepared in Poland. The national government chose Rogoziński to administer the oath to all those who wished to take part in the Uprising of 1863, and when it began he was recruited into the ranks of the nation's defenders as a chaplain. The uprising failed, but the chaplain made it safely through to Galicia where he intended to settle. However, he was caught and, as a politically compromised person, he was imprisoned in Olomuniec where he stayed for eleven months." (Kruszka IV, p. 62) Upon release from prison and obtaining a passport, he went to Paris for a few years. Eventually he meet Bishop Dubois of Galveston, TX who enlisted him as a missionary to Texas in 1871. After a few years he left Texas for the Polish settlements in Wisconsin. He came to the Archdiocese of Milwaukee on 28 May 1877. Before assuming the pastorate of St. John's, Princeton, he served at St. Michael's, Beaver Dam (1877-1878) and Northeim. After Princeton, Reverend Rogoziński was assigned to the parish of St. Stanislaus, Bishop & Martyr, Milwaukee as an assistant to Rev. Górski for a year and a half. On December 11, 1885, he was assigned as pastor of St. Hedwig's Catholic Church, Milwaukee. He remained there until his death on 16 May 1901(Archdiocese of Milwaukee Archives). Father Rogożiński is credited with building the new church along with building harmony among the parishioners and was known as the "builder of St. Hedwig's". (Diamond Jubilee 1946 p. 22). Father Rogożinski "died at 11 o'clock last Thursday night after an illness of three weeks, during which his constant attendant has been his assistant, Rev. Bronislaus Celichowski. Father Rogożinski was born in Russian Poland sixty-six years ago."

"The body of the dear priest lay in state amidst a profusion of flowers within the sanctuary of the church (St. Hedwig's Milwaukee), which had been draped in black and purple, until Tuesday when the funeral took place.

"At 9 o'clock the office of the dead was chanted by a number of the assembled priests of whom at least a hundred from all parts of the city, state and surrounding states had gathered to pay the last tribute to their departed brother. After the office of the dead was finished, Archbishop Katzer began the pontifical funeral mass. Rev. Victor Zaręczny of Beaver Dam preached a eulogistic sermon in Polish and the body of the dead priest was conveyed to the hearse, the following priests acting as pallbearers: Rev. Fathers A. Pradzynski, S. Nowricki, Gordon, S. Kaperski, F. Wojtalewiecz, P. Szulerecki. The various societies marched in procession back of the hearse as far as Broadway bridge, returning from there to the church.

"When the body arrived at the Polish cemetery (St. Adalbert's), Eighth

Avenue, Rev. John Szukalski preached another sermon and then the body was consigned to its last resting place." (Obit The Catholic Citizen May 1901). He had been a priest for forty-one years. On 6 June 1885 Rev. Rogożiński declared his intention of being a U.S. citizen. From the application we learn that he was born in 1836 in the Russian partition of Poland and emigrated to Wisconsin n 1871 via the Port of New York.

Rev. Clement Rogożinski first served in Maulbery (Praha), TX 1871-1875 before coming to St. Michael Church, Beaver Dam, WI in 1877. From 1887 onward he was a stockholder and on the board of directors of the Polish Publishing Co., Chicago, IL. Rev. Rogożinski was associated with the Congregation of the Resurrection Apostolate in the United States.

Courtesy of Krentz Collection
Rectory built by Rev. Rogożiński in 1881

Father Rogozinski
From "Diamond Jubilee St. Hedwig" p. 22

Courtesy of RFK

Here lies
Rev. Ludwig
Klemens
Rogozinski
Pastor of St. Jadwiga Parish
Born 24 August 1835
?, Poland
died 16 May 1901
St. Adalbert Cemetery, Milwaukee, WI

6. Rev. Emanual John Słowikowski   1 June 1884-17 Sept 1886

Reverend Emanual John Słowikowski arrived at St. Peter's parish, Stevens Point to assume the pastorate in 1882. It was during his tenure at St. Peter's that a new rectory was built for $2500. In 1883 the parish of St. Peter's was incorporated. He remained in Stevens Point until 23 May 1884. He then became the pastor of St. John's, Princeton from 1 June 1884 and remained until 17 September 1886.

From September 1886 until 1888 he is associated with St. Stanislaus Kostka Church, Chicago, IL. From 1887 onward he was a stockholder in the Polish Publishing Co., Chicago, IL. Rev. Słowikowski was associated with the Congregation of the Resurrection Apostolate in the United States.

In 1888 Rev. Emanual Jan (John) Słowikowski began ministering to St. Wojciech (Adalbert) Parish, Berea, OH (Diocese of Cleveland) and remained there until 1890. Rev. Kruszka refers to him as an "ex-Capuchin." Later he is mentioned to be one of a number of very short-term Polish pastors of St. Stanisław, B & M Church, New York City.

"In April 1895, the wandering monk, Fr. Emanuel Słowikowski, passed away in Stary Sącz, Poland He was from Stary Sącz by birth and, having saved some money in America, offered it to his countrymen in his last testament. Indeed, he bequeathed his entire fortune for public use of the inhabitants of his family town of Sącz, including such projects as the restoration of the parish church, the canonization of Blessed Kinga, a hospital for the poor, and also a scholarship fund for the poor school youth of Stary Sącz. His inheritance was executed and completed in March 1899 by the district court in Stary Sącz, which paid out all bequests where appropriate, and the scholarship fund of over 80,000 crowns was sent to the governor's office in Lwów for further distribution." (Kruszka vol. IV p. 18).

Stary Sącz is a small town in the south of Poland and dates from the 13th century. In 1257 Bolesław the Chaste, Prince of Kraków and Sandonierz, gave the Sącz district to his wife, Kinga. The origins of the town are associated with the creation of the parish church of St. Elizabeth of Hungray (Kinga's aunt). In the town Bl. Kinga established a Monastery of Poor Clare nuns and after the death of her husband in 1297, she permanently lived in the convent. Among her numerous achievements, history tell us she tirelessly worked for the canonization of the martyred Stanisław, Bishop of Kraków, just as Fr. Słowikowski worked for the canonization of Bl. Kinga. Within her Poor Clare monastery on Holy Trinity hill are the tombs of St. Kinga and Queen Jadwiga, the wife of King Ladisław the Short, the mother of King Casimir the Great and the great-grandmother of St. Jadwiga of Sącz. St. Kinga died 24 July 1292. Pope Alexander XIII beatified her in 1690 and Pope Benedict XIII declared her Patroness of Poland Lithuania. During a ceremonial mass in Stary Sącz on 16 June 1999, Pope John Paul II canonized Blessed Kinga. Her feast day is kept on 24 July.

Fr. Emanual John Słowikowski most likely is buried in the "Old Cemetery" at the church of Ss. Roche and Sebastian at the south end of Stary Sącz.

Rev. E. J. Slowikowski

From "Diamond Jubilee St. Peters" p. 15

7. Rev. Victor Zaręnczny   17 Sept 1886-17 Apr 1887

Reverend Victor (Wiktor) Zaręnczny (Zaręczny, Zaręczni) was born in Lwow, Galicia, Austrian partition of Poland on 3 December 1841. He was ordained on 22 July 1868 at Bielsko Biała, Galicia, Austria after completing his theology studies there by Alojzy Pukalski, Bishop of Tarnów. He did parish work in the Diocese of Tarnów until 1873 when he emigrated to the United States of America. He arrived in the U.S. on 15 November 1873. "The young priest began his American mission among his fellow Poles in the community of Berea, OH (just east of Cleveland). He organized and was the first pastor of St. Adalbert parish (one of the oldest Polish parishes between Buffalo and Chicago and still functioning today). While there, Zaręczny was also responsible for building the first brick church (which was dedicated in September 1875), for purchasing land for the parish cemetery, and for establishing a parish school." (www.pgsnys.org/Poland/priest_36.html).

In 1879 he was a curate at St. Stanisław, B & M parish, New York City.

"In February 1884, Zaręczny was appointed pastor of yet another St. Adalbert parish, this time in Pittsburgh, PA. Since a church had not yet been built, he held services at the neighboring St. John the Evangelist church, but immediately began raising monies to purchase land for the parish's own structure. His stay in this community lasted until June of that same year.

By 1886 he is pastor of Ss. Cyril & Methodius, Eaton, WI. On 17 September 1886 he assumed his duties as pastor of St. John the Baptist Church, Princeton and remained there until 17 April 1887. It was during his pastorate that the present church building was being planned.

After leaving Princeton, he went to work in the Diocese of Buffalo (NY). He returned once again to Wisconsin and for a short time served at Holy Trinity, Pine Grove, WI. He is associated with Ss. Cyril & Methodius, Eaton, WI in 1885, New Denmark and Montpelier, WI, St. John the Baptist, Belmont (Portage Co.). In 1891 he was appointed the pastor of Assumption church in the Black Rock area of the Diocese of Buffalo, NY. This was followed by a three year pastorate at St. Adalbert parish in the Diocese of Buffalo, NY. In 1895 he is found again in Wisconsin, serving in St. Michael's, Beaver Dam 1895-1901, St. Casimir Kenosha 1901-1902; St. Hyacinth's, Milwaukee 1902-1903 and Berlin. "In 1903 he left Wisconsin to accept a position as chaplain of the new St. Mary of Nazareth Hospital in Chicago, IL. Between 1908-1910 he is back in Wisconsin, first as pastor of St. Michael, Berlin then at St. John the Baptist, Belmont. It was here that he spent his last days, dying on 7 November 1918 at the age of 76." (www.pgsnys.org/Poland/priest_36.html). In 1911 he became the chaplain of Holy Family Hospital, Chicago soon after the death of Rev. Edward Rajnerta. He remained in this position until he died. On 21 July 1918 Rev. Zaręnczny celebrated his golden sacerdotal jubilee of ordination. He died at 9 o'clock in the evening after a brief illness and receiving the Holy Sacraments. He was buried Monday 11 November 1918 at 9 a.m. from St. Mary of Nazareth Hospital chapel and was interred in St. Adalbert's Cemetery, Niles, Illinois, lot 14, Block B, section 17. (Obit Dziennik Chicagoski 9 Nov 1918)

Courtesy of RFK
Tombstone of Rev. Victor Zaręnczny
Section 7, Block B, Lot 14
St. Adalbert Cemetery
Niles, IL
(There was no separate head stone for Rev. Zaręnczny)

Rev. Edward Rejnert
1852 + 1911 Priest 37 years
Rev. Romualo Macott
1829 + 1915 Priest 63 years
Rev. Wiktor Zarenczny
1841 + 1918 Priest 50 years
Rev. Ulrich Martel
1835 + 1921
Hail Mary

8 & 14. Rev. John Quirin Zieliński   17 Apr 1887-Oct 1891
                                              19 Mar 1897-25 Sep 1899

Reverend John Quirin (Quintius, Kwiryn) Zieliński was born 3 June 1844 in Grabienice, Konin district, Kalisz Province, in the Russian partition of Poland. "He entered the monastery in 1861 and completed classical studies (rhetoric) at the high school of the Bernardine Fathers in Skęp, Płock Province. He then studied in the high school in Przasnysz, and finally, in 1864, after the monastery was dissolved, he went abroad. He first stayed in Paris for a year, then in Oleta and Ajaccio on the island of Corsica where he studied philosophy and theology for the priesthood for four years. He was ordained in Ajaccio on June 24, 1867. He supplemented his studies as a priest in Rome at the college of St. Bartholomew all'Isola on the Tiber island. After a year there, he went to Paris, where he was (even during the siege of Paris by the Prussians) a priest 'for everything' (pretre habitué) from 1868 to 1879. Then he worked half a year in Belgium in the nunciature, and then for a half a year as a chaplain to the Sisters in Antwerp. From October 1879 to November 1882, he worked as a 'free priest' at the cathedral in Munich." (Kruszka v.IV p. 52).

At the invitation of Reverend Jacek Gulski Rev. Zieliński immigrated to Wisconsin and worked as an assistant at St. Stanislaus, Bishop & Martyr Church, Milwaukee for nine months. He was assigned as pastor of St. Michael's, Beaver Dam on 4 July 1884 and stayed until April 1887.

On 17 April 1887 he assumed the pastorate of St. John the Baptist Parish, Princeton and remained there until October 1891. In May 1887 Timothy Paul moved the wooden church structure west a lot or two to give room for the new church. The new edifice was to be started immediately. (PR vol. XXI #20, 2 June 1887). There was a delay in the start of construction of the new church because Architect Druiding's plans and specifications could not be executed by local builders. It was decided to wait until the next spring to start construction. (PR vol. XXI #27 27 July 1887). It was during Rev. Zieliński's pastorate that the corner stone of the present church was laid and the present church building was nearly completed with dedication on 4 November 1888 at 10 o'clock a.m. In September 1888 a new bell was blessed by Fr. Zieliński and installed in the church tower. He is responsible for the opening of the first Catholic school in Princeton in the basement of the church in December 1888 with Mr. Julius Zaczek as the teacher. There were approximately 100 students enrolled in the school. In 1887 there were 217 Polish families, 15 German and Irish families in the parish for a total of 1282 souls.

He was transferred to St. John the Baptist Parish, Menasha in May 1892 and received into the Diocese of Green Bay by Bishop Sebastian Messmer on 15 March 1893. On 1 May 1894 he was assigned to St. Peter's Parish, Stevens Point during a stormy period in the history of the parish. Rev. Zieliński "bought a new roof for the church, expanded the choir to 26 places, made the rectory more attractive, and enlarged the cemetery and divided it into plots." (Kruszka vol. IV p. 19). In September 1896, he secured the "Polish School Sisters of St. Joseph" of Stevens Point to teach in the parochial school. On 18 October 1896, before vespers, the church and rectory burned to the ground. Rev. Zieliński brought a law suit against Sigmund Hitter, owner of the Polish newspaper of Stevens Point, the "Rolnik" for the amount of $5000 for alleged libel. Rev. Zieliński seemed to have much trouble with his parishioners of St. Peter's. There was even an assassination attempt on his life. Starting on 18 November 1896, he took a five month leave of absence. Upon resuming his priestly duties, he was assigned back to St. John the Baptist Parish, Princeton on 19 March 1897 and remained there until 25 September 1899. His last assignment was to take up the pastorate of St. Hyacinth's Parish, Antigo 25 September 1899. Here he died of a heart attach on 22 March 1907 and is buried in Queen of Peace Cemetery, Antigo.

From "Catholic Church in Wisconsin" p. 721
Reverend John Quirin Zieliński

Courtesy of RFK
Reverend Zielinski's grave in Queen of Peace Cemetery, Antigo, WI

Courtesy of RFK

John Quirin Zielński
Born 3 June 1844
In Grabienice in Poland
Died 22 March 1907
As pastor of St. Hyacinth's Parish
In Antigo, Wis
Rest in Peace

9. Rev. Richard Frank   Dec. 1891-21 Oct 1892

Reverend Richard (Ryszard) Frank was the successor of Rev. Zieliński. He came to Princeton in December 1891 and stayed until his death on 21 October 1892. Rev. Frank was born in Soznowice, Prussian partition of Poland, on 2 September 1842. The Archbishop of Poznań, Poland, [later Cardinal] Miecislaus Ledochowski ordained Rev. Frank on 12 March 1868. He emigrated to the United States and eventually to Wisconsin in March 1890. He served as pastor at New Franken, WI from January 1891 to December 1891. He was then transferred to St. John the Baptist Church, Princeton. He was responsible for rebuilding and furnishing the old church into a home for the School Sisters of St. Francis who were teaching in the parochial school. He is also provided costly chalices and vestments for the church at his own expense. However his most significant achievement during his short tenure at St. John's was paying off the entire debt from the newly built church. According to the Princeton Times Republic Rev. Frank died on Saturday, 22 October 1892. "He was found by Mr. Keller lying prostrate in front of the door of his residence. One foot was partially on the lower step, and his body lay partly on the ground and partly on the walk in front of the step. In one hand was a bunch of keys that were used in locking both the church and the residence. He had apparently started to lock the church, a duty usually performed by him, and fell as he was found. There was no evidence of a struggle, but it would rather appear that death came very soon, if not instantly. Dr. Racek being called pronounced it a case of apoplexy. Esquire Myers being notified soon impaneled a coroner's jury composted of the following persons: Martin Manthey, Valentine Czarnetzki, A.M. Priske, Stanislaus Maslowski, Jacob Junker and Henry Drill. After making a thorough examination the jury rendered the following verdict: "That the said Richard Frank was found dead at the front door of the parsonage and that there were no marks of violence found upon the body; and that he died by the visitation of God, in a natural way and not otherwise. Rev. Richard's habits were peculiar. He lived entirely alone. His death must have occurred early in the evening previous to the discovery of his body in the morning. When found the frosty dew had collected on his clothing showing he had laid there alone and unnoticed for several hours." (PTR vol. XXVI #41 27 Oct 1892). At the time there was speculation as to the cause of death, but it would appear it was a heart attach. His body lay in state in the church from Sunday, 23 October until the funeral on 25 October. Rev. Q. Zieliński celebrated the Solemn Requiem High Mass. Rev. J. Holzknecht preached a sermon in Polish; Rev. J. Czarnowski preached a sermon in German; and Rev. H. Gulski of Milwaukee had the graveside service in Polish. Priests from the surrounding area attended the funeral. He is buried in the parish cemetery. From 1894 until 1973 the School Sisters of St. Francis cared for Rev. Frank's grave.

From "Catholic Church in Wisconsin" p. 1026
Reverend Richard Frank

Courtesy of RFK
Here lies
the body of Father R. Frank
died
21 October 1892
Please say
A Hail Mary

Courtesy of RFK
Rev. Richard Frank's grave in St. John the Baptist Catholic Cemetery, Princeton

10. Rev. Joseph Froehlick   2 Nov 1892-12 Dec 1892

The tenth pastor of St. John the Baptist Catholic Church was **Rev. Joseph Boniface Froehlick (Froelich)**. Joseph Boniface was born in February 1860 in Fulda, Germany. He received his education there before immigrating to the United States in 1877. He entered the St. Vincent's Seminary near Pittsburgh, PA. Later in 1884 he entered St. Francis de Sales Seminary, Milwaukee. Archbishop Heiss of Milwaukee ordained him 29 June 1885. He started his priestly ministry as an assistant at the St. Francis Xavier Cathedral, Green Bay until 1888. He became pastor of the parish at Greenville before coming to St. John's, Princeton on 2 November 1892. However, he remained in Princeton only until 15 December 1892. After leaving Princeton he was pastor at Random Lake, St. Anna, WI, Campbellsport and North Greenfield. He retired from active ministry around 1900 taking up residence at Menasha where he pursued his hobby of organ building and gardening. He died 17 April 1919 at St. Elizabeth's Hospital, Appleton. He is buried in plot 162 in St. Mary's Cemetery, Menasha, WI. (Long, p. 157).

In the 1900 U.S. census Rev. Froehlick is living in North Greenfield, WI. His mother, Margaret Froehlich (born 1829, emigrated to Wisconsin in 1889) was living with him at this time.

From "Catholic Church in Wisconsin" p. 524
Rev. Joseph Boniface Froehlick

Courtesy RFK
Rev. Froelick's grave in St. Mary's Cemetery, Menasha, WI

Courtesy of RFK
Rev. Froelick's grave in St. Mary's Cemetery, Menasha, WI

Here rests in God
Rev. Joseph Froelich
Born 14 February 1860
Died 17 April 1919
In the 34th year of his
Priestly position

11. Rev. Victor Lebjecki   15 Dec 1892-1 Jan 1894

Rev. Victor Mansuetus Lebjecki (Lebiecki, Lebieski, Lebecki) was born in 1828 in the Russian partition of Poland. He was educated, ordained, and did priestly ministry in Poland before coming to the United States. It is known he was a priest of the Diocese of Lublin, Poland and already ordained by 1868. He emigrated in August 1884 to the United States of America via the Port of New York. He "held pastorates in the diocese of Green Bay as follows: Amherst Junction (Fancher) [Our Lady of the Scapular] Portage Co. December 1889; Wausau, St. Michael's, 1891; Princeton (Green Lake Co.)

[St. John the Baptist] 15 December 1892 to 21 October 1894 when he retired. Listed in one source as administrator at Sharon in 1897. Died at Stevens point, April 27, 1898." (Long, p. 246). Rev. Lebjecki was at St. Michael's, Wausau when the construction of the new church was undertaken. He celebrated the first Mass in the basement of the new church. When the church was completed it was consecrated by Bishop Katzer.

On 9 October 1890 Rev. Lebjecki declared his intention of becoming a citizen of the U.S. and became a naturalized citizen on 21 November 1893 in Portage County, Wisconsin.

From "Catholic Church in Wisconsin" p. 721
Reverend Victor Lebjecki

Courtesy of RFK

Here sleeps in the Lord
Rev. Victor Lebiecki
Born
6 March 1838
ordained a priest
21 May 1853
Diocese of
Lublin, Poland
Died
27 April 1896
Rest in Peace
Please say
A Hail Mary
St. Peter's Cemetery, Sec. 3. Stevens Point, WI

12. Rev. Adam Lopatto   1 Jan 1894-1 Feb 1896

Reverend Adam S. Lopatto (Łopata) was born 20 October 1859 in Lithuania. He was ordained to the priesthood on 25 November 1884 in Kovno, Lithuania. He arrived in the Port of New York on 2 February 1893. He left Bremerhaven on the ship "Salier" for New York. Rev. Lopatto became the 12th pastor of St. John the Baptist Catholic Church, Princeton on 1 January 1894 and stayed until 1 February 1896. He is most remembered for securing the services of the School Sisters of St. Francis (Milwaukee, WI) to teach in the parochial school beginning in 1894.

Like many priests at this time he spent short periods of service in a number of parishes in Wisconsin once he was accepted into the Diocese of Green Bay in 1894. Besides Princeton, he is associated with the parishes in Holy Trinity, Pine Grove; Sacred Heart, Marinette; and St. Stanislaus, Hofa Park. The order he served in each parish is not known, except for his time in Princeton. He spent a few weeks in pastoral work at Sacred Heart, Two Rivers before leaving the Diocese of Green Bay early in 1898. "One letter indicates that he served for a time in the Diocese of Peoria; another account that he died as chaplain of St. Mary's Villa at Elmhurst, PA on April 18, 1946." (Long, p. 256). The U.S. Census records for 1910, 1920. 1930 list Rev. Lopatto as living in Old Forge, Lackawanna County, PA. It is known he was serving Holy Family parish, Wilkes-Barre, PA 22 September 1898 to 1905; St. Mary's, Wanamie, PA 1905 to 11 July 1906; St. Mary's, Blossburg, PA 12 July 1906 to 4 November 1907; St. Stanislaus, Old Forge, PA 5 November 1907 to 9 March 1911; St. Anthony's Lithuanian parish, Forest City, PA 10 March 1911 to 25 August 1914; St. Michael's Lithuanian parish, 1703 Jackson St., Scranton, PA 26 August 1914 to 1930. From 1930 until his death on 8 April 1946 at age 86, Rev. Lopatto was chaplain at St. Mary's Villa (Elmhurst, PA) for the Poor Sisters of Jesus Crucified and the Sorrowful Mother at their Motherhouse there. "Althought his health during those years was weak and fragile, he fulfilled his duties to the best of his abilities." (Sr. Marie Elizabeth, letter 2011). The Poor Sisters of Jesus Crucified and the Sorrowful Mother is a Lithuanian Congregation devoted to "charity towards the neighbor, exercised in caring for the aged, orphans, and in instructing children in schools." (McCarthy, 1958, p.300).

Rev. Lopatto was buried on 11 April 1946 in St. Mary's Villa Cemetery on Blue Shutters Road, Elmhurst, PA (back grounds of the Villa property), row 8 #44. The inscription on his tombstone is in Lithuanian.

Courtesy of Susan Danna
Rev. Lopatto's tombstone in St. Mary's Villa Cemetery, Elmhurst, PA

Rev. Adam S. Lopatto

13. Rev. Louis Starostzick   1 Feb 1896-19 Mar 1897 (1 yr 1 mo)

Reverend Louis (Ludwig) Charles Maria Starostzick (Starościk, Storoskicz), son of Joseph S. Starostzick and Louisa Frank, born 6 October 1853 in Kieferstaedtel (Sosnicowie), Silesia, Germany, the son of a high school teacher. He was 40 years old when he emigrated to the United States. He left Bremen on 18 January 1894 on the ship "Furst Bismarck" for the United States. Rev. Starostzick succeeded Rev. Lopatto as pastor of St. John the Baptist Church, Princeton on 1 February 1896 and remained until 19 March 1897.

He was educated in Gleiwitz, Germany; studied philiosphy and comparative languages at the University of Leipzig and Wroclaw from 1874-1884; in 1887; he passed the exam for organist and director of choir for municipal churches; and theology at the University at Kraków, Poland and Wroclaw, Poland. He was recruited by Archbishop Messmer of Milwaukee for ministry in Wisconsin. He finished his priestly studies at St. Mary Seminary, Cincinnati, OH 1890-1894. He received tonsure and lower orders on 9 June 1894; subdeaconate on 12 June; and deaconate on 15 June, 1894. Archbishop William Elder ordained Louis Starostzick to the priesthood on 19 June 1894 in Cincinnati, OH for the Diocese of Green Bay at the age of forty. His first Mass was celebrated in the Chapel of the Good Shepherd, Green Bay, Wisconsin. The Bishop of the Diocese of Green Bay assigned him as the pastor of Sacred Heart, Marinette on 7 July 1894. He was only there for a few months before being transferred to Antigo to found St. Hyacinth's Parish on 20 September 1894 (while in Antigo, he lived at St. John's Rectory). After his tenure at St. John's, Princeton, he served St. Joseph's, Steven Point beginning in March 1897; Our Lady of the Scapular, Fancher in 1898(Long, p. 366); St Josaphat, Oshkosh 1 March to May 1900; St. Francis Xavier, Portage in 1901; chaplain, St. Mary's Hospital, Racine November 1906-October 1908; St. Michael's, St. Michael, WI October 1908 – December 1910; St. Anthony Convent, North Greenfield, WI 1912; chaplain, St. Mary's Hospital, Columbus 1918 (Archdiocese of Milwaukee Archives). Rev. Starostzick died at St. Mary's Hospital, Columbus, WI on 1 September 1923. He had been in failing health and spent the last two weeks of his life confined to his bed in the hospital. His funeral Requiem Mass was celebrated on Tuesday, 4 September 1923 at 9:30 a.m. with interment in the Catholic cemetery section of Hillside Cemetery, Columbus, WI (Obit 23 Sept 1923 Columbus Democrat). It should be noted Rev. Starościk was a relative of Rev. Richard Frank and a famous musician. (Kruszka vol. IV p. 81).

In 1905 the Diocese of Superior was created and the boundaries of the three dioceses in Wisconsin changed. The Dioceses of Milwaukee, Green Bay and La Crosse were arranged to follow the county borders instead of rivers. This eliminated the concept of a county being divided between two dioceses. Also, priests serving in these areas had the choice of which diocese they wished to minister in. In 1905 Princeton was incorporated into the Archdiocese of Milwaukee, following the county boundaries. Before this, Princeton, as well as Berlin being on the Fox River, was part of the Diocese of Green Bay.

On 19 March 1897 Reverend Quintius Zielinski accepted the pastorate of St. John the Baptist Church, Princeton for the second time. He remained at Princeton until 25 September 1899.

Courtesy of RFK
Grave of Rev. Louis (Ludwig) Starostzick
St. Jerome Cemetery, Columbus, WI

Courtesy of RFKrentz

St. Jerome Cemetery, Columbus, WI

Here lies
Rev.
Ludwig Starostzich
Born 6 Oct 1853
Wschlesien Germany
Died 1 Sept 1923
Columbus, Wis
RIP

ST. JOHN THE BAPTIST CATHOLIC CHURCH
PRINCETON, WISCONSIN
ARCHDIOCESE OF MILWAUKEE
(1905-1945)

15. Rev. Sigmund Woźńy   **25 Sep 1899-3 Nov 1909**

The next pastor of St. John the Baptist church, Princeton was **Reverend Sigmund (Zygmunt) Woźńy**. He was born in Austrian Poland on 16 August 1861 son of Joseph Woźńy and Maria Gajesko. He was educated in Wadowice, Kraków and Vienna. He studied theology for the priesthood at Louvain, Belgium where he received minor orders on 6 June 1884 from Rt. Rev. Peter Goosens Archbishop of Malines. He was made subdeacon of 8 June 1884 by the same prelate. On 20 December 1884 was ordained deacon by Rt. Rev. Vanden Branden de Reeth and on 28 June 1885 ordained to the priesthood by Rt. Rev. Aegidius Junger of the Diocese of Nesqually, Washington for the Diocese of Leavenworth (KS). (Archdiocese of Milwaukee Archives). Rev. Woźńy immigrated to the United States and first worked in the Diocese of Leavenworth, Kansas for a year, moved on to the Diocese of Peoria (IL) for five years before incardinated into the Diocese of Green Bay in January 1891. While in the Diocese of Peoria, he was pastor of St. Hyacinth's parish, LaSalle, IL (9 August 1886-15 January 1892). From 1891 to 1894 he was the pastor of St. Peter's, Stevens Point. On 1 May 1894 he was pastor of St. Hyacinth's parish, Antigo, WI for four months. Briefly pastor of St. John the Baptist, Menasha in 1894. Then he moved to St. Casimir, Cleveland, OH and became the first permanent pastor. The local Bishop assigned him to establish the Catholic parish of the Assumption of the Blessed Virgin Mary in Grafton, OH. From 1896 to 1897 he traveled in Mississippi, California, Oregon, Washington, Vancouver Island, British Columbia and Alaska. He returned to Wisconsin in 1897 and became pastor of St. Michael's, Berlin (May 1897 to 25 September 1899); and then St. John the Baptist, Princeton 25 September 1899 to 3 November 1909.

During his pastorate of St. John's, Princeton "he renovated the church beautifully and made an effort to have it consecrated." (Kruszka vol. IV p.

81). On Sunday, 17 July 1904 a fire broke out in the priest's sacristy of St. John's church around 3 in the afternoon. Although the fire didn't spread, it did cause considerate damage to the priestly vestments. The damage was estimate at about $1000. Rev. Woźny was a good friend of the great Polish historian and priest, Rev. Wacław Kruszka of St. Wencelaus Church, Ripon, WI. Rev. Kruszka was often the preacher for Forty-Hours Devotions, etc. at. St. John's. Rev. Woźny ordered the best altars for the church in 1901 from Hashner's of LaCrosse, WI at a cost of $1,900. They were installed for Christmas of 1901. In 1906 a new pipe organ was purchased from Ross-Scheft-Wienman of Milwaukee at a cost of $1,450. It was blessed and dedicated on 11 June 1906 with a musical recital by William Bayez of Milwaukee. At the dedication of the organ, Rev. Wozńy had Prof. Raphael Baez (organist of St. John the Evangelist Cathedral, Milwaukee) preside at the organ concert; soprano Miss C. Malek of Milwaukee sang both in Polish and English; along with the participation of the Weinkauf's orchestra. Rev. Wacław Kruska, pastor of St. Wencelaus Church, Ripon, WI preached. (PR 14 June1906).

After his tenure in Princeton, he came under the jurisdiction of the Archdiocese of Milwaukee at his request with the remapping of the diocesan boundaries in 1905. After serving in Princeton, he was assigned to St. Michael's, Beaver Dam (1909-1911) and from 14 March 1913 to 30 May 1922 to St. Stanislaus Kostka Church, Berlin where he served for a number of years. According to the 1920 U.S. census his housekeeper in Berlin was Helen Szweda. Rev. Wozńy was the first priest in Berlin to own an automobile. " The priest was a familiar figure here (Berlin) because he used a bell signal on his automobile to help him in driving it. He was near-sighted and the bell warned him when his car was not going straight." (Ironwood Daily Globe). In the fall of 1922 he retired from active ministry, but resided in Berlin, WI. He died suddenly Thursday morning, 3 June 1937 at Yates Memorial Hospital, Berlin, WI where he was a patient for only four days. Death was due to advanced age. He was a priest for 52 years. His funeral was held at St. Michael's church, Berlin on Tuesday, 8 June 1937 at ten o'clock a.m. with the Very Reverend Monsignor John A. Mikolajczak, pastor of St. Hedwig's, Milwaukee and former pastor of St. Michael's, Berlin officiating. Archbishop Stritch preached the sermon. Interment was in St. Michael's cemetery. (Obit 7 Jun 1937 Oshkosh Northwestern p. 7).

Courtesy of Krentz Collection

Interior of St. John's as it looked pre-1909

From Diamond Jubilee St. Peters" p. 16

Rev. Zygmunt Woźny

Courtesy of RFK
Rev. Wozny's grave in St. Michael's Catholic Cemetery, Berlin, WI

16. Rev. Joseph C. Knitter   3 Nov 1909-22 Apr 1915

  Rev. Joseph Conrad Knitter was born 26 November 1879 in Kruszyn (Diocese of Chełmno), Prussian Poland, son of Alexander Roman Knitter and Marianne Bielawa. He emigrated to the United States of America in 1888 via the Port of New York with his family. He attended Marquette University High School, Marquette University, and completed his studies for the priesthood at St. Francis De Sales Seminary, Milwaukee. Archbishop Sebastian Messmer ordained Joseph Conrad Knitter to the priesthood on 19 June 1904. He celebrated his First Mass on Sunday, 26 June 1904 in St. Casimir's Church, Milwaukee, WI. (Archdiocese of Milwaukee Archives). His first assignment was as an assistant priest at St. Vincent de Paul Church for a short time. He then became an assistant pastor at St. Josaphat's

Milwaukee for five years. He did register for the World War I draft according to the 1917-1918 draft records. On 28 June 1906 Rev. Knitter declared his intention of becoming a U.S. citizen. He was sponsored by Stanley E. Czerwinski and Mathias G. Ball. He was an assistant pastor at St. Josaphat Church, Milwaukee from 1907 to 1909.

In 1910 he received his first pastorate—that of St. John the Baptist, Princeton, WI. "At the January 1910 meeting, Father Knitter authorized the building of a new barn. In those days the parishioners came to church by horse and buggy and in winter, the horses were kept warm in the barn during Mass. (The horse barn was located along the south side of the cemetery and just west of the convent). There were 200 men at the meeting. In 1911 electric lights were installed in the sisters' home, priest's home, and the school." (Krystofiak 1987, p.5). In February 1914 new Stations of the Cross were installed in St. John the Baptist Catholic Church, Princeton. At the dedication of the Stations in mid-February 1914 Rev. Knitter was assisted by Father Wenta, Milwaukee and Father Lepinski, Neshkoro (PR 26 Feb. 1914). Also in 1914, St. John's installed a new 700 pound bell. Several months earlier the parish installed a 1400 pound bell. The new one conforms in tone with the larger one. Rev. Knitter held a blessing ceremony for each bell.

On 13 April 1915 Rev. Knitter was made pastor of St. Mary of Czestochowa parish in Milwaukee where he remained for thirty-four years. In recognition for his services to the Church, Pope Pius XII made Rev. Knitter a domestic prelate of the Pontiff with the title of Right Reverend Monsignor. At the age of 69, Rev. Knitter died in the St. Mary of Czestochowa rectory on Saturday 13 August 1949 from a heart attack.

"The solemn funeral Mass was celebrated by Auxiliary Bishop Roman R. Atkielski in the presence of Archbishop Moses E. Kiley. Bishop Atkielski gave the final absolution. Frs. John A. Wieczorek and Michael Stanczak were deacon and sub-deacon of the Mass, Fr. Joseph E. Emmenegger was the master of ceremonies. The deacons of honor were Msgr. R. J. Kielpinski and Msgr. F. P. Reilly. Burial was beside the graves of his parents in Holy Cross cemetery.

"Msgr. Knitter's funeral Mass followed the office of the Dead. His body was taken into the church at 4 p.m. Tuesday, to lie in state until the funeral services began. There were vigils by all the parish societies." (Obit, Herald Citizen vol. 79, no. 38, 20 Aug 1949)

Rev. Knitter's sister, Angeline Knitter lived with him at the rectory of St. Mary of Czestochowa parish. He, also had a sister who was a member of the

School Sisters of Notre Dame, Sister M. Joseph Knitter, SSND at Elm Grove and a married sister, Mrs. Bernadine Osmanski, of Crivitz, WI.

From Memorial card 1949
Rt. Rev. Msgr. Joseph C. Knitter

Courtesy of RFK
The Knitter Family Plot in Holy Cross Cemetery, Milwaukee, WI

Courtesy of RFK
The grave of Monsignor Knitter in front of the Knitter Family Tombstone in Holy Cross Cemetery, Milwaukee, WI

17. Rev. Joseph S. Chylewski   22 Apr 1915-5 Dec 1923

Rev. Joseph Stanisław Chylewski was born 11 March 1876 in Gostoczyn, Poznań, Wielkopolskie, Poland. He was the son of George Chylewski (born 1850) and Agnieszka Deja (born 13 January 1855, died 16 May 1889 in Allegan, Allegan County, MI, daughter of Albert Deja and Maryanna Modrzejewska). He was the oldest of eight children. His parents married in 1875. The Chylewski family emigrated to the United States of America in October 1879 and settled in Detroit, MI.

Rev. Chylewski graduated from the Gregorianum, Rome, Italy with a Ph.D. degree and was ordained on 20 May 1900 in Rome by Rt. Rev. Appetelli for the Archdiocese of Detroit. (Archdiocese of Milwaukee Archives). From 1900 to 1901 he was a professor at the Theological Polish Seminary, Detroit, MI. In March 1903 he was incorporated into the Archdiocese of Milwaukee where he had been a curate at St. St. Hedwig's since 29 August 1901. Subsequently he served as pastor of Immaculate Conception Church, Manitowoc, WI on 26 March 1903; assistant at St. Josaphat, Milwaukee, 1904; pastor of St. Stanislaus, Racine, 1906, St. Joseph Orphan Asylum, 30 September 1909, pastor of St. Stanislaus, Bishop & Martyr, Milwaukee, 1913; pastor of St. John the Baptist, Princeton 1915; professor at Pio Nono College, Milwaukee, December 1923 and resigned in Spring of 1926; and chaplain of St. Mary Hospital, Milwaukee 28 March 1927 until his death 24 March 1928. His funeral was held on 27 March 1928 at St. Casimir Church, Milwaukee with burial in St. Adalbert's Cemetery. (Obit Catholic Herald 7 April 1928)

On 29 June 1906 in Milwaukee, WI Rev. Joseph Chylewski declared his intention of becoming a U.S. citizen. His sponsors were Balaslaus E. Goral and Rev. Paul Gosa.

On 19 September 1918 Rev. Chylewski registered for the World War I draft while he was pastor of St. John the Baptist Catholic parish, Princeton. At this time his sister, Johanna Chylewski was his housekeeper.

During Rev. Chylewskis's tenure as pastor of St. John the Baptist, Princeton, WI, the parish purchased land from Frank Wyse and Joe Wyse for $1700. In 1916 the old wooden church (the Schools Sisters residence) was razed and the materials used to construct a new convent for the teaching sisters. To meet the expenses of the parish, each pew holder was assessed an extra $5 per year.

Courtesy of Krentz Collection
School Sisters convent circa 1916

From Diamond Jubilee St. Stanislaus B&M p. 22
Rev. Dr. Joseph S. Chylewski

Courtesy of RFK
Rev. Chylewski's grave in St. Adalbert's Cemetery, Milwaukee

Here Lies
SP Reverend Doctor Joseph
Chylewski
Born 19 March 1876
Died 24 March 1928
Rest in Peace

18. Rev. Thomas V. Jankowski   6 Dec 1923-5 Mar 1942

Rev. Thomas Victor Jankowski born 3 November 1882 in Mt. Carmel, PA, son of Michael Jankowski and Anna Shuda. In 1890 the family moved to Milwaukee, WI. He was the oldest of eight children. His father was a grocer in Milwaukee and lived on Becher Street, Milwaukee. He attended parochial schools and eventually enrolled in St. Francis de Sales Seminary, Milwaukee, WI. He received minor orders on 16 March 1907 at the Salesianum, Milwaukee from Archbishop Sebastian Messmer; ordained a subdeacon 4 April 1908, deacon 5 April 1908 and priesthood on 14 June 1908 by Archbishop Fox for the Archdiocese of Milwaukee..

His first priestly assignment was as assistant pastor at St. Hedwig Catholic Church, Milwaukee, WI 22 June 1908; assistant at St. Michael, Beaver Dam 16 July 1909; assistant at St. Stanislaus B & M, Milwaukee 3 November 1909; assistant at Ss. Cyril & Methodius, Milwaukee 6 July 1910; assistant at St. Patrick, Janesville April 1911; assistant at St. Joseph, Fond du Lac May 1911. It appears he left the Archdiocese of Milwaukee between 1911 and 1914. Upon his return, he was appointed rector of St. James, Neshkoro, WI in 1914 along with the mission church of St. Patrick's, Princeton, WI. While at Neshkoro he registered for the World War I draft on 12 September 1918 in Montello, WI. His assignment in Neshkoro lasted until 6 December 1923 when he succeeded Rev. Joseph Chylewski as pastor of St. John the Baptist Catholic Church, Princeton. During his time in Princeton Hattie Cybela was his housekeeper.

During the long tenure of Rev. Jankowski, the St. John the Baptist parish voted to continue to have a tuition free school. In 1929 the road in front of the church was paved with concrete. The parish voted to assess each pew holder $2.00. In 1930 the church installed the beautiful stained glasses windows. Each window was donated either by an individual family or by a parish organization. During Rev. Jankowski's tenure there were improvements made to the St. John's campus: cement pavement leading from the Main Street to the sidewalks, and entrance to the cemetery.

"The first parish report to all the pew holders was made in 1935. A new blueprint of the cemetery was made and all the markers on the cemetery were to be numbered. ….in 1938 a new floor was installed in the church." (p. 6 Krystofiak 1987). On 4 July 1936 Fr. Tom broke ground for connecting the waterworks and sewerage systems with St. John's church, rectory, the school and the Sisters' home. "According to the custom of the Church, it is the duty and privilege of the priest to turn the first shovel of dirt on a project of this kind; and as Father Tom was due to leave Sunday for his annual retreat, work was started on the Fourth." (9 July 1936 PTR). "At the St. John's Catholic School the installation of the water works and sewer has made a decided improvement. Wash rooms with white tiled walls have been built on both sides of the rear hall and equipped with white furnishings. A bubbler place in this hall, between the two school room doors, is easily accessible to all children." (10 Sept 1936 PTR). Other improvements were made at the same time, mainly (1) a semi-circular concrete walk was made outside the rear door; (2) 2 new black iron fire escapes were added to the church building; (3) ventilators were installed at intervals under the classroom floors to dispel the dampness of the floors; (4) an outside door was cut into the intermediate grade classroom; and the Sisters' home and the rectory had the trim painted cream and brown. (10 Sept 1936 PTR).

Up to this time, Rev. Thomas V. Jankowski was the longest serving pastor of St. John the Baptist Catholic Church, Princeton—18 years. He was affectionately known as "Father Tom." He was the first priest in Princeton to own an automobile. On Monday, 3 August 1930 at 1:30 p.m. he had the honor of driving the first car over the new bridge over the Fox River amidst cheers from the workmen and spectators. (7 Aug 1930 PTR). In February 1932 Rev. Jankowski won a suit against the National Retailers Company. On 27 November 1931 His car caught fire which was partially destroyed and the insurance company denied liability. Thus Fr. Jankowski sued the insurance company. The case was settled when the insurance company agreed to paying for the repair of Rev. Jankowski's automobile. (4 Feb 1932 PTR).

Fr. Tom was only 59 when he died at 4 a.m. Thursday, 5 March 1942 in the rectory at St. John the Baptist Catholic church. Father Tom has been in poor health for some time. About two weeks earlier he caught a severe cold and was apparently too much for his weakened heart. He died in his sleep. (Obit 5 Mar 1942 PTR).

"All creeds and all walks of life were represented by those who paid their last respect to the Reverend Thomas Jankowski.. during the time his remains lay in state in the church Sunday afternoon and evening and at the services Sunday and Monday.

"Long years of service to his parishes in Princeton and in Neshkoro, his many pleasant business and social contacts throughout this area, his interest in sports, and his jovial disposition had won him the sincere friendship and respect of thousands of persons who feel that his passing is a personal loss.

"The church was filled Sunday afternoon as the remains were brought in. Rev. Anthony Czaja, pastor of St. James church at Neshkoro and St. Patrick's here, gave a discourse in English. Until late in the evening there was a constant procession of mourners to view the remains.

"It is estimated that close to 1200 persons packed the church to capacity for the funeral services which commenced at 10:30 Monday morning. The services will be remembered as the most elaborate ever held in the St. John the Baptist church. Almost every business place in Princeton was closed Monday morning during the time of the services.

"Archbishop Moses Kiley and Msgr. Roman Atkielski of Milwaukee honored the service by their presence. Those talking part were: Rev. Joseph Platta of Ripon, who celebrated the mass; Rev. A. Czaja of Neshkoro, deacon of the mass; Rev. David Reagan, Berlin, sub-deacon; Rev. Walter Polewski, Milwaukee, as master of ceremonies; Rev. Geo. Lehman of Milwaukee, acting as thurifer; Rev. Dowling of Berlin who gave the sermon in English; Rev. John Bonk of Berlin, who gave a sermon in Polish; Rev. Stephen Szczerbiak of Beaver Dam and Rev. John Banka of Plainfield, who said mass at the side altars." (12 Mar 1942 PTR)

Numerous area priests and priests from other parts of Wisconsin attended the funeral. Burial of Rev. Thomas Jankowski took place in St. Adalbert's Catholic Cemetery, Milwaukee at 3:30 Monday afternoon. Members of the Catholic Order of Forests of St. John's acted as pallbearers. There were: Vince Weiske, John Kasierski, John Kalupa, Stanish Resheske, Frank Nicodem, Stanish Kozlowski.

Rev. Thomas Jankowski

Courtesy of RFK
Rev. Jankowski's grave in St. Adalbert's Cemetery, Milwaukee, WI

ST. JOHN THE BAPTIST CATHOLIC CHURCH
PRINCETON, WISCONSIN
DIOCESE OF MADISON
(1945 to present)

19. Rev. Dr. Francis S. Karwata   19 Mar 1942-8 Jun 1956

Ignace Karwata and Mary Karwata, the parents of Rev. Karwata, emigrated from Pozńan, Poland and settled in the Chicago area in 1881. Reverend Francis S. Karwata was born 29 January 1893 in Chicago, IL. He attended the local parochial school of St. Hedwig Catholic Church, Chicago. He entered St. Stanislaus College, Chicago in 1906 where he completed both high school and college studies, graduating in 1911. He joined the Congregation of the Resurrection and was professed on 11 March 1913 in Rome, Italy. He completed his studies in Philosophy, Theology and Canon Law at the Pontifical Georgian University, Rome. Upon graduation, he received a Doctor of Philosophy degree and Licentiate in Sacred Theology CUM LAUDE. He was ordained to the priesthood in the Basilica of St. John Lateran, Rome 28 April 1918 by His Eminence Basil Cardinal Pompili.

After ordination he returned to Chicago on 14 August 1919 and was assigned to teach at the Resurrectionist College of St. Stanislaus from 1919-1921 and again in 1923-1924. During 1922 he was assigned to St. Mary of the Angels Church, Chicago, IL. On 2 May 1924 Reverend Francis S. Karwata left the Congregation of the Resurrection (Janas, p. 197 1991) and was incardinated into the Archdiocese of Milwaukee. Archbishop Sebastian Messmer appointed him Spiritual Director of the Big Brothers of the Holy Name Society. He served as assistant pastor of St. Hedwig Catholic Church, Milwaukee, WI 1924-1925; assistant pastor of St. Casimir Catholic Church, Milwaukee, WI 1925-1930 under Pastor, Reverend Rudolph Kielpinski; 1930-1940 Professor of Polish at Marquette University and taught at Messmer High School, Milwaukee, WI; 1933 appointed administrator of Our Lady of Pompeii parish, Kenosha, WI; 1940-1942 pastor of St. Stanislaus, Bishop & Martyr Catholic Church, Racine, WI.

While in Racine, "his ability as an organizer began to show itself.. He had the interior of the church redecorated, installed a new pipe-organ, paid off all parish debts, and left enough money in the parish treasury for future needs. He kept close watch over his parochial school so that it always maintained the highest standard. For the young people of the parish he organized The Newman Club. Apart from his parochial duties, he took an active part in both national and church affairs, speaking on the radio and at public meetings." (Souvenir Program Sacerdotal Silver Jubilee).

Rev. Dr. L.M. Long wrote the following about Fr. Karwata. "The faithful of his parish know him as a zealous, self-sacrificing man, one truly devoted to his God and to his people. He needs no human praise; his works speak for themselves. In a short time, he renewed the parish school, and put the parish on a financially sound basis. The children attend the parochial school without paying any tuition. Knowing well that youth must be led, he organized a Newman Club for the young people of his parish. He frequently conducts lectures for its members on religious, literary, social, and other sundry topics. He is ever mindful of the spiritual welfare of those entrusted to his care, always doing his utmost to minister to their spiritual needs.

"He is a man of God, endowed with a clear mind and a heart full of courage; a humble, patient, zealous priest. Truly, he is the good steward of the Lord's household. It is little wonder, then, that those who know him, learn to love him.

"Besides the priestly virtues that he possesses, the Rev. Dr. Francis Karwata has a thorough knowledge of various languages. His eloquent sermons convince, edify, and find their mark in the mind and heart of the listener." (Souvenir Program Saccerdotal Silver Jubilee).

On 19 March 1942 Reverend Francis S. Karwata was appointed pastor of St. John the Baptist Catholic Church, Princeton where he remained for fourteen years. During his tenure in Princeton, WI. In addition to his pastoral duties he served as Judge on the Diocese of Madison Matrimonial Court from 1946 to 1956. Rev. Karwata won the respect and devotion of, not only his parishioners, but of the local town's people as well. He was the last of the truly cultured, Polish priests to serve St. John the Baptist parish. He had the ability to make everyone feel important. At the Solemn High Mass of Thanksgiving on 11 December 1938, on the occasion of the golden anniversary of the establishment of St. Hedwig's Catholic Church, Chicago, IL, Fr. Karwata served as deacon. His Excellency, the Most Rev. Stanislaus V. Bona was the celebrant and the Rev. Edward Morkowski, CR the subdeacon. St. Hedwig's was Rev. Karwata's home parish.

On 28 June 1942 Rev. Dr. Karwata lead the parish in paying tribute to the forty-two parish sons in the Armed Forces of the Nation. Dedication of the American flag and blessings of the service banner and honor roll, took place after the eight o'clock High Mass. Benediction followed the dedication ceremonies. The members of St. John's Court of the Catholic Order of Foresters received Holy Communion in a body during the Mass.

The service flag had 41 blue stars in honor of the living soldiers and one gold star in memory of Pvt. Leonard Kozlowski who was killed in action on Corregidor, 29 April 1942. The honor roll was inscribed with the names of all the boys in the armed forces of the United States.

"The flags and the honor roll are the gifts of St. John's Court C.O.F., St. Anne's Court C.O.F., and of all the parishioners who contributed by their donations to the patriotic and religious causes." (25 Jun1942 PTR). The flags and the honor roll were discarded during the Rev. Eberhardy pastorate.

On 8 June 1956 Rev. Francis S. Karwata left St. John's, Princeton to become the pastor of Our Lady of the Lake, Green Lake, WI. He remained in Green Lake until his death on 2 October 1959 from cancer. On Sunday, 4 October 1959 his body lay-in-state in Our Lady of the Lake Catholic Church, Green Lake, WI until the time of the funeral at 10:30 Monday, 5 October

Courtesy of the Krenz Collection
Interior of St. John's showing the Honor Roll Flag

1959. His good friend, Rev. Julian F. Bieniewski (St. Michael's Catholic Church, Berlin, WI) recited the rosary at 7:30 p.m. Sunday. The Office of the Dead was chanted by the priests on Monday morning, 5 October 1959. A Solemn Requiem Highs Mass was celebrated at 11 a.m., 5 October with the Rev. Julian F. Bieniewski Celebrant. His Excellency William P. O'Connor, Bishop of Madison gave the Absolution. After the funeral services on Monday his body was taken to the Joseph Wojciechowski Funeral Home, Chicago, IL. There was a rosary at the funeral home Monday evening for family and friends in Chicago. A Solemn Requiem High Mass was celebrated on Tuesday, 6 October 1959 at St. Hedwig Catholic Church, Chicago (his home parish). Burial followed in the family plot in St. Adalbert Catholic Cemetery, Niles, IL.(Obit 8 Oct 1959 PTR). Rev. Julian F. Bieniewski, Pastor of St. Michael's, Berlin, WI and his housekeeper; Conrad Napierala of Princeton, WI; and Roger F. Krentz, Ph.D. Princeton, WI attended the funeral and burial in Chicago, IL.

Rev. Francis S. Karwata

Courtesy of RFK
The Karwata Family tombstone
Section 7, Block D, Lot 2
St. Adalbert Cemetery
Niles, IL

Courtesy of RFK
Tombstone of Rev. Francis S. Karwata who is buried next to his
parents in the family plot in St. Adalbert Cemetery, Niles, IL

20. Rev. Josef V. Cieciorka   8 Jun 1956-18 Jun 1969

The Reverend Josef V. Cieciorka died 30 May 1998 at the age of 94 in West Palm Beach, Florida. He had been living there the past few years. A funeral Mass was held at 11 a.m. Thursday, 3 June 1998 at St. Peter Catholic Church, Stevens Point, WI with The Most Reverend William H. Bullock, Bishop of Madison, officiating. Burial followed in St. Peter Parish Cemetery, Stevens Point, WI.

Josef V. Cieciorka, son of Constantine Cieciorka and Bertha Ziolkowski, was born on 12 March 1904 in Hatley, near Stevens Point, WI. He was one of nine children in the family. His parents were married 4 February 1901 at St. Peter's Catholic Church, Stevens Point, WI. He attended St. Peter Catholic School, Stevens Point, St. Bonaventure High School, Pulaski, WI, St. Paul Seminary, St. Paul, MN and St. Francis de Sales Seminary, Milwaukee, WI. The Most Reverend Joseph Pinten, Bishop of Grand Rapids (MI) ordained Josef V. Cieciorka to the priesthood on 2 February 1930 at St. Francis de Sales Seminary, Milwaukee, WI.

During his priestly ministry, Rev. Josef V. Cieciorka served as assistant pastor at St. Hedwig Catholic Church, Milwaukee, WI; St. Stanislaus Catholic Church, Milwaukee, WI; and St. Mary Magdalen Catholic Church, Milwaukee, WI. He served at St. Stanislaus Catholic Church, Racine, WI as assistant pastor before being appointed pastor at St. Barnasbas Catholic Church, Mazomanie, WI. He was assistant pastor at St. Stanislaus, Bishop & Martyr, Racine between 1940-1942 while Rev. Francis S. Karwata was the pastor.

When the Diocese of Madison was erected in 1945, he elected to remain with the new diocese. On 8 June 1956 he was assigned the pastorate of St. John the Baptist Catholic Church, Princeton, WI, where he served until retiring on 18 June 1969. His other ministries included: CYO director for Racine (WI) for 20 years; Boy Scout director for the Diocese of Madison for 12 years; Displaced Persons director for the Diocese of Madison for 10 years; notary for the Matrimonial Tribunal and a synodal judge in the Diocese of Madison. (Obit 8 June 1988 Stevens Point Journal).

While at St. John the Baptist Catholic Church, Princeton, WI, Reverend Josef V. Cieciolka revived the parish picnics on the Sunday following the Feast of the Assumption in August; built and paid for the new school; started a basketball program; had a new organ donated, money banked for the rectory and church renovation; started Mother of Perpetual Help devotions; encouraged membership in the Ladies Rosary Society and the Men's Holy Name Society; started Catholic Scouting in the parish; started the weekly church bulletin; started the Parish Council and the School Board and Education Committee.

Rev. Cieciorka was the only pastor of St. John's to have assistant priests assigned to help him in this large parish. They were: Rev. Thomas Sosinski (1960-1963); Rev. George Horath (1963-1965; Rev. Timothy Gericke (1965-1966); and Rev. Richard Lesniak (1966-5 months).

Courtesy of RFK
St. Peter's Cemetery, Sec. 3. Stevens Point, WI

Courtesy of the Krentz Collection
Catholic school built by Rev. Cieciorka

21. Rev. John B. Eberhardy   18 Jun 1969-19 Jun 1979

John B. Eberhardy born 19 March 1910, son of Peter Eberhardy and Catherine Phillippi, in Hewitt, Wisconsin. He attend St. Michael's parochial school, Hewitt, WI, the St. Nazianz Salvatorian Seminary and College, and philosophy and theology at St. John's University, Collegeville, MN. He was ordained to the priesthood on 3 May 1936 by Bishop William R. Griffin in St. Joseph Cathedral, LaCrosse, WI. His first Holy Mass was celebrated at St. Michael's, Hewitt, WI on 5 May 1936.

He served as associate pastor at St. Aloysius Church, Sauk City, WI May 1936 to June 1937; associate pastor at St. John Church, Marshfield, WI June 1937 to June 1938; associate pastor at St. Charles Church, Chippewa Falls, WI June 1938 to Jun 1939. He was appointed pastor of St. John the Baptist Church, Cooks Valley, WI June 1939 to June 1942; pastor of St. Joseph Church, Sinsinawa June 1942 to August 1947; pastor of Mary Help of Christians Church, Glen Haven, August 1947 to August 1953; pastor of St. Francis Xavier Church, Cross Plains, WI August 1953 to February 1964; pastor of St. Joseph Church, Argyle, WI February 1964 to June 1965; pastor of St. Mary's Church, Mineral Point, WI June 1965 to 18 June 1969; pastor of St. John the Baptist Church, Princeton, WI 18 June 1969 to 19 June 1979. He retired on 19 June 1979 and continued to live in Princeton.

He died 18 August 1992 in Princeton, WI. A Mass of Christian Burial was held on Friday, 21 August 1992 at 11 a.m. in St. John the Baptist Catholic Church, Princeton with Bishop George Wirz and Rev. Dale Grubba officiating. Burial was in St. Michael's Catholic Cemetery, Hewitt, WI (Wood County).

Fr. Eberhardy had the dubious honor of implementing Vatican II. He, along with numerous of his colleagues, plunged headlong into this implementation with little or no preparation nor understanding of the council documents and the spirit of Vatican II. Thus St. John the Baptist parish lost the communion rail, statues, banners etc. all donated by hard working Polish farmers in the name of Vatican II. The documents do not mention the need or wish to discard anything from the churches. If the Council demanded this, St. Peter's in Rome would be empty. He even wanted to rip out the three altars, but the will of the parishioners prevailed and they are still there today. After donations of our forefathers were discarded, new objects of less artistic, historic, and lesser devotional value took their place, but were asked to be donated—all for Vatican II. Fr. Eberhardy believed he was acting according to Vatican II, but I personally doubt if he ever studied the documents, especially on worship and the worship space. He could have saved the parish much consternation, money and loss of faith.

Courtesy of Diocese of Madison Archives
Rev. John B. Eberhardy

Courtesy of RFK
St. Michael's Cemetery, Hewitt, WI

22. Rev. Philip Krogman   19 Jun 1979-17 Jun 1985

Rev. Philip John Krogman is one of two living priests who have or are serving St. John's, Princeton, WI. He was born 13 June 1934 in Bloomington, WI. He attended St. Mary's parochial school in Bloomington, WI and the Salvatorian Seminary, St. Nazianz, WI. He studied philosophy and theology at St. John University, Collegeville, MN. He was ordained to the priesthood on 28 May 1960 by Bishop William P. O'Connor in St. Raphael Cathedral, Madison, WI.

He has served the Diocese of Madison in a variety of capacities. His parish duties include: associate pastor St. Raphael Cathedral, Madison 1960-1964; associate pastor St. Mary, Platteville 1964-1968; pastor of Our Lady of Hope, Seymour with the mission of St. Peter, Elk Grove 4 Feb. 1970-June 1975; pastor of St. Rose of Lima, Cuba City 18 June 1975-18 June 1979; pastor of St. John the Baptist, Princeton 19 June 1979-17 June 1985; pastor of St. Henry, Watertown 18 June 1985-15 June 1987; pastor of St. Rose of Lima, Cuba City 16 June 1987-17 June 1991; pastor of Immaculate Conception, Kieler 18 June 1991-29 June 1999; pastor of St. Paul, Evansville 30 June 1999-17 October 2000; and pastor of Our Lady of the Lake, Green Lake 18 October 2000 to present. He has held additional offices through the years of his priestly service: teacher at St. Pius X 1866-1968; chaplain Newman Apostolate at UW-Platteville 1968-1972; dean of Grant County 1975; Madison Diocesan Spiritual Moderator 1981-1983; Clergy Development Committee 1994-1996.

23. Rev. Dale W. Grubba   18 Jun 1985-to present

Rev. Dale William Grubba was born 24 August 1940 in Portage, Wisconsin. Bishop William P. O'Connor ordained him a priest on 28 May 1966 in St. Raphael Cathedral, Madison, WI. He served on the faculty of Holy Name Seminary after ordination; associate pastor pro tem at St. Cecilia, Wisconsin Dells 20 June 1978 – June 1981; pastor of St. Joseph, Waterloo 11 June 1981-17 June 1985; pastor of St. John the Baptist, Princeton 18 June 1985 to present and linked with St. James Neshkoro 14 June 2000. He also served as dean of Marquette and Green Lake in August 1998 on the Presbyeral Council to 2008.

Rev. Grubba is an avid NASCAR fan and closely follows the racing circuit. He has written several books on the subject. Among his books are: <u>Testament of the Weekend Warrior</u> (1997); <u>Golden Age of Wisconsin Auto Racing</u> (2000); <u>Return of Elijah, a Wisconsin Dells Thriller</u> (2001); and <u>Alan Wuliwicki NASCAR Champion Against All Odds</u> (2009).

Through his tenure at St. John the Baptist, Princeton, he has maintained an active parochial school and has kept the church in remarkable condition, both interior and exterior. In 2010 Rev. Grubba celebrated his 25th year at St. John's, his 10th year with St. James Catholic Church, Neshkoro, WI and his 70th birthday. The parishes gave him an all-expense paid trip to the Holy Land.

On your walls, Jerusalem, I have set my watchmen to guard you.
Common of Pastors

CONCLUSION

1. Longest service to the parish:
   Fr. Dale Grubba 25+ years
   Fr. Thomas Jankowski 18 years 3 months
   Fr. Francis S. Karwata 14 years 2 months 20 days
   Fr. Josef Cieciorka 13 years 10 days
   Fr. Sigmund Woźny 10 years 1 month 1 week

2. Shortest service to the parish:
   Fr. Adam Bukowski 1 month
   Fr. Joseph B. Froehlick 1 month 10 days
   Fr. Joseph Szpecht 7 months
   Fr. Victor Zaręnczny 7 months
   Fr. Victor Lebjecki 1 year 2 weeks

3. Oldest priest assigned to the parish
   Fr. John B. Eberhardy 59 years old
   Fr. John Ignatius Zawistowski 55 years old
   Fr. Josef V. Cieciorka 52 years old
   Fr. Richard Frank 49 years old
   Fr. Francis S. Karwata 49 years old
   Fr. Klemens Rogożiński 44 years old

4. Youngest priest assigned to the parish
   Fr. Joseph Froehlick 32 years old
   Fr. Victor Zaręnczny 35 years old
   Fr. Zygmunt Woźny 38 years old

5. First priest to serve in the parish that was born in the US
   Fr. Thomas Victor Jankowski (Pennsylvania 1882)

6. Priests buried in the cemetery
   Fr. Richard Frank
   Fr. Michael Doro (priest son)

7. Most educated
   Rev. Dr. Joseph S. Chylewski
   Rev. Dr. Francis S. Karwata

8. Former Religious Order priests
   Fr. Januarius Czarnowski [Franciscan]
   Fr. Fr. John Ignatius Zawistowski [Discalced Carmelite]
   Fr. Klemens Rogoziński [Bernardine*] after 1887 associated with the Congregation of the Resurrection Apostolate]
   Fr. Emanual John Słowikowski [Capuchin, later associated with the Congregation of the Resurrection Apostolate]
   Fr. John Quirin Zieliński [Bernardine]
   Fr. Francis S. Karwata [Congregation of the Resurrection]

9. Missionary Apostolics
   Fr. Januarius Czarnowski
   Fr. Adam Bukowski

10. Priests that were related
    Fr. Richard Frank and Rev. Louis Starostzick were cousins.

11. First Wisconsin born priest to serve as pastor at St. John's.
    Rev. Josef V. Cieciorka born in Hatley, WI (Portage County).

12. Unkown burial places of priests
    Fr. Joseph Szpecht
    Fr. Adam Bukowski

13. Priests buried outside of Wisconsin
    Fr. Victor Zaręcnczny—St. Adalbert Cemetery, Niles, IL
    Fr. Francis S. Karwata—St. Adalbert Cemetery, Niles, IL
    Fr. Emanuel Słowikowski—Stary Sącz, Poland
    Fr. Adam Lopatto—St. Mary's Villa Cemetery, Elmhurst, PA

14. Priests buried in Wisconsin
    Fr. Januarius Czarnowski—St Stanislaus Cemetery, Berlin
    Fr. John Zawistowski—St. John Cemetery, Highland
    Fr. Klemen Rogoziński—St. Adalbert Cemetery, Milwaukee
    Fr. John Zieliński—Queen of Peace Cemetery, Antigo
    Fr. Richard Frank—St. John Cemetery, Princeton
    Fr. Joseph Froehlich—St. Mary Cemetery, Menasha
    Fr. Victor Lebjecki—St. Peter Cemetery, Stevens Point
    Fr. Louis Starostzick, St. Jerome Cemetery, Columbus
    Fr. Sigmund Wożny—St. Michael Cemetery, Berlin
    Fr. Joseph Knitter—Holy Cross Cemetery, Milwaukee

Fr. Joseph Chylewski—St. Adalbert Cemetery, Milwaukee
Fr. Thomas Jankowski—St. Adalbert Cemetery, Milwaukee
Fr. Josef Cieciorka—St. Peter Cemetery, Stevens Point
Fr. John Eberhardy—St. Michael Cemetery, Hewitt

15. Years of priestly ordination at the time of death
Fr. Rev. Josef V. Cieciorka 68 years
Fr. Adam Łopata 62 years
Fr. John Eberhardy 56 years
Fr. Sigmund Woźny 52 years
Fr. Victor Zaręnczny 50 years
Fr. Joseph C. Knitter 45 years
Fr. John Ignatius Zawistowski 43 years
Fr. Clement Rogożiński 40 years
Fr. Quintius Zieliński 40 years
Fr. Francis S. Karwata 38 years
Fr. Joseph B. Froehlick 34 years
Fr. Thomas V. Jankowski 34 years
Fr. Victor Lebjecki 30+
Fr. Ludwig Starostzick 29 years
Fr. Joseph S. Chylewski 28 years
Fr. Januarius Czarnowski 25 years
Fr. Richard Frank 24 years

Unknown: Fr. Joseph Szpecht, Fr. Adalbert Bukowski, and Fr. Emanuel Słowikowski.

16. Age of the priests at the time of death
Fr. Josef V. Cieciorka 94 years
Fr. Adam Łopata 86 years
Fr. John B. Eberhardy 82 years
Fr. Victor Zaręnczny 77 years
Fr. Sigmund Woźny 76 years
Fr. Victor Lebjecki 70 years
Fr. Ludwig Starostzick 70 years
Fr. Joseph C. Knitter 70 years
Fr. John Ignatius Zawistowski 67 years
Fr. Clement Rogożinski 66 years
Fr. Quintius Zieliński 63 years
Fr. Francis S. Karwata 63 years
Fr. Thomas V. Jankowski 60 years
Fr. Joseph B. Froehlick 59 years

Fr. Januarius Czarnowski 53 years
Fr. Joseph S. Chylewski 52 years
Fr. Richard Frank 50 years

Unknown: Fr. Joseph Szpecht, Fr. Adalbert Bukowski, and Fr. Emanuel Slowikowski.

* When the Franciscans were reformed in the 15th century by St. Bernardine of Siena, that Franciscan branch became known as Bernardines. The Bernardines followed a strict observance of the Franciscan rule.

APPENDIX A

Diocese of Green Bay

Rev. Joseph Szpecht	Feb. 1875-Sept 1875
Rev. Januarius Czarnowski	Sept. 1875-July 1877
Rev. Adalbert Bukowski	July 1877-Aug.1877
Rev. John Ignatius Zawistowski	Sept. 1877-Dec. 1879
Rev. Clement Rogoziński	Dec. 1879-June 1884
Rev. Emanuel John Słowikowski	1 June 1884-17 Sept 1886
Rev. Victor Zaręnczny	17 Sept 1886-17 Apr 1887
Rev. Quintius Zieliński	17 Apr 1887-Oct 1891
Rev. Richard Frank	Dec 1891- 21 Oct 1892
Rev. Joseph B. Froehlick	2 Nov 1892-15 Dec 1892
Rev. Victor Lebjecki	15 Dec 1892-1 Jan 1894
Rev. Adam Łopata	1 Jan 1894-1 Feb. 1896
Rev. L. Starostzick	1 Feb 1896-19 Mar 1897
Rev. Quintius Zieliński	19 Mar 1897-25 Sep 1899

Archdiocese of Milwaukee

Rev. Sigmund Woźny	25 Sep 1899-3 Nov 1909
Rev. Joseph C. Knitter	3 Nov 1909-22 Apr 1915
Rev. Joseph S. Chylewski	22 Apr 1915-5 Dec 1923
Rev. Thomas V. Jankowski	6 Dec 1923-5 Mar 1942

Diocese of Madison

Rev. Francis S. Karwata	19 Mar 1942-8 Jun 1956
Rev. Josef V. Cieciorka	8 Jun 1956-18 Jun 1969
Rev. John B. Eberhardy	18 Jun 1969-19 Jun 1979
Rev. Philip Krogman	19 Jun 1979-Jun 1985
Rev. Dale W. Grubba	Jun 1985-

APPENDIX B

Bishops who had jurdictistion over St. John the Baptist Catholic Parish, Princeton, WI

Diocese of Green Bay 1875-1905

Most Reverend Frederick X. Katzer 1886—1891
Most Reverend Sebastian G. Messmer 1892—1903
Most Reverend Joseph J. Fox 1904—1914

Archdiocese of Milwaukee 1905-1945

Most Reverend Sebastian G. Messmer 1903—1930
Most Reverend Samuel A. Stritch 1930—1939
Most Reverend Moses E. Kiley 1940—1953

Diocese of Madison 1945-Present

Most Reverend William P. O'Connor 1946—1967
Most Reverend Cletus F. O'Donnell 1967—1992
Most Reverend William H. Bullock 1993—2003
Most Reverend Robert C. Morlino 2003—present

APPENDIX C

Other Parishes Served by Priests Who Ministered in Princeton

Ahnapee
St. Raphael
Fr. J. Zawistowski

Antigo
St. Hyacinth
Fr. Q. Zieliński
Fr. Z. Woźny
Fr. L. Starostzick

Argyle
St. Joseph
Fr. J. Eberhardy

Beaver Dam
St. Micahel
Fr. T. Jankowski
Fr. K. Rogoziński
Fr. W. Zaręnczny
Fr. Z. Woźny
Fr. Q. Zielinski

Belmont
St. John the Baptist
Fr. W. Zaręnczny

Berlin
St. Stanisław Kostka
Fr. J. Czarnowski
Fr. W. Zaręnczny
Fr. Z. Woźny

Berlin
St. Michael
Fr. Z. Woźny
Fr. W. zarenczny

Campbellsport
St. Matthew
Fr. J. Froehlick

Chippewa Falls
St. Charles
Fr. J. Eberhardy

Cooks Valley
St. John the Baptist
Fr. J. Eberhardy

Cross Plains
St. Francis Xavier
Fr. J. Eberhardy

Cuba City
St. Rose of Lima
Fr. P. Krogman

Eaton
Ss. Cyril & Methodius
Fr. W. Zaręnczny

Elk Grove
St. Peter
Fr. P. Krogman

Evansville
St. Paul
Fr. P. Krogman

Fancher
Our Lady of the Scapular
Fr. V. Lebjecki
Fr. L. Starostzick

Fond du Lac
St. Joseph
Fr. T. Jankowski

Glen Haven
St. Mary Help of Christians
Fr. J. Eberhardy

Green Bay
St. Francis Xavier
Fr. J. Froehlick

Green Lake
Our Lady of the Lake
Fr. F. Karwata
Fr. P. Krogman

Greenville
Immaculate Conception
Fr. J. Froehlick

Highland
St. John Nepomuc
Fr. J. Zawistowski

Hofa Park
St. Stanisław
Fr. A. Łopata

Hull
St. Casimir
Fr. J. Czarnowski

Janesville
St. Patrick
Fr. T. Jankowski

Kieler
Immaculate Conception
Fr. P. Krogman

Kenosha
St. George (?)
Fr. W. Zaręczny

Madison
St. Raphael
Fr. P. Krogman

Manitowoc
Immaculate Conception
Fr. J. Chylewski

Marinette
Sacred Heart
Fr. A. Łopata
Fr. L. Starostzick

Marshfield

St. John
Fr. J. Eberhardy

Mazomanie
St. Barnabas
Fr. J. Cieciorka

Menasha
St. John the Baptist
Fr. W. Woźny

Milwaukee
St. Casimir
Fr. F. Karwata

Milwaukee
Ss. Cyril & Methodius
Fr. T. Jankowski

Milwaukee
St. Hedwig
Fr. K. Rogoziński
Fr. T. Jankowski
Fr. F. Karwata
Fr. J. Cieciorka
Fr. J. Chylewski

Milwaukee
St. Jozaphat
Fr. J. Knitter
Fr. J. Chylewski

Milwaukee
St. Mary Magdalene
Fr. J. Cieciorka

Milwaukee
St. Stanisław B&M
Fr. K. Rogoziński
Fr. Q. Zieliński
Fr. J. Cieciorka
Fr. J. Chylewski
Fr. T. Jankowski

Milwaukee
St. Vincent de Paul
Fr. J. Knitter

Milwaukee
St. Mary of Częstochow
Fr. J. Knitter

Mineral Point
St. Mary
Fr. J. Eberhardy

Montpelier
St. Mary of the Seven Dolors
Fr. W. Zaręczny

Neshkoro
St. James
Fr. T. Jankowski

Neshkoro
St. James
Fr. D. Grubba

New Denmark
Holy Trinity
Fr. W. Zaręczny

New Franken
St. Kilian
Fr. R. Frank

North Greenfield
St. Matthias
Fr. J. Froehlick

Northeim
St. Casimir
Fr. K. Rogożiński

Oshkosh
St. Josaphat
Fr. L. Starostzick

Oshkosh
St. Mary
Fr. J. Zawistowski

Pine Grove
Holy Trinity
Fr. W. Zaręczny
Fr. A. Łopata
Fr. L. Starostzick

Platteville
St. Mary
Fr. P. Krogman

Poniatowski
St. Joseph
Fr. A. Bukowski

Portage
St. Francis Xavier
Fr. L. Starostzick

Princeton
St. Patrick
Fr. T. Jankowski

Racine
St. Stanisław
Fr. F. Karwata
Fr. J. Cieciorka
Fr. J. Chylewski

Random Lake
St. Mary
Fr. J. Froehlick

Sauk City
St. Aloysius
Fr. J. Eberhardy

Seymour
Lady of Hope
Fr. P. Krogman

Sinsinawa
St. Joseph
Fr. J. Eberhardy

St. Ann
St. Ann
Fr. J. Froehlick

St. Michael
St. Michael
Fr. L. Starostzick

Stevens Point
St. Peter
Fr. J. Czarnowski
Fr. A. Bukowski
Fr. E. Słowikowski
Fr. Q. Zieliński
Fr. Z. Wożny

Stevens Point
St. Joseph
Fr. L. Starostzick

Two Rivers
St. Luke
Fr. J. Zawistowski
Fr. A. Łopata

Waterloo
St. Joseph
Fr. D. Grubba

Watertown

St. Henry
Fr. P. Krogman

Wausau
St. Michael
Fr. V. Lebjecki

Wisconsin Dells
St. Cecilia
Fr. D. Grubba

APPENDIX D

Graves of other priests associated with St. John the Baptist, Princeton, WI.

Courtesy of RFK
Rev. Sosinski's grave in St. Stanislaus Kostka Cemetery, Berlin, WI
Curate at St. John the Baptist)1960-1963) under Rev. Josef V. Cieciorka.

Courtesy of RFK
Rev. Michael Doro, priest son of St. John the Baptist, Princeton, WI buried in the parish cemetery.

BIBLIOGRAPHY

Archdiocese of Milwaukee Archives. Priests folders: Rev. L. Starostzick. Rev. V. Zarenczny, Rev. J. Chylewski. Rev. J. Knitter, Rev. T. Jankowski, Rev. C. Rogozinski, Rev. S. Wozny. Milwaukee, WI.

Bolek, F.(1943). Who's who in Polish America. NY : Harbinger House.

Centennial Story of St. Anthony's Parish Highland, Wisconsin 1860-1960. (1960). Highland, WI : St. Anthony's Catholic Parish.

Diamond jubilee of St. Hedwig, 1871-1946. Milwaukee, WI : St. Hedwig's Church.

Diamond jubilee St. Peter's Congregation Stevens Point, Wisconsin 1876-1951. Stevens Point, WI : St. Peter's Parish.

Diamond jubilee St. Stanislaus 1866-1941. Milwaukee, WI : St. Stanislaus B & M Parish.

Heming, H.H. (1896). Catholic Church in Wisconsin : a history of the Catholic Church in Wisconsin from the earliest time to the present day. Milwaukee, WI : Catholic Historical Publishing Company.

Hoffmann, M.M. (1937). The Church founders of the Northwest: Loras and Cretin and other Captains of Christ. Milwaukee, WI : The Bruce Publishing Company.

Ironwood Daily Globe, Ironwood, MI, Friday 4 June 1937.

Karwata, F.S. (1943). Souvenir Program Sacerdotal Silver Jubilee of Rev. Francis S. Karwata at St. John the Baptist Parish, Princeton, WI. n.p.

Kruszka, X.W. (1905). Historya Polska w Ameryce: Poczatek, wzrost I trozwój dziejowy osad polskich w Pólnocnej Ameryce (w Stanach Zjednoczonych i Kanadzie). Milwaukee, WI : Drukiem Spólki Wydawniczej Kuryera (13 volumes).

Kruszka, X. W. (1924). Siedem siedmoileci, czyli pód wieky zyciz : pamietnik i prazyczynek do historji polskiej w Ameryce. Milwaukee, WI : Nakladem autora (2 volumes).

Kruszka, X.W. (2001). A history of Poles in American to 1908. [4 parts]. Washington, D.C. : The Catholic University of American Press.

Krystofiak, A. (1987). St. John the Baptist Church, Princeton, Wisconsin : a century of dedication love and caring 1887-1987. n.p.

Kuzniewski, A.J. (1973). Faith & fatherland: an intellectual history of the Polish immigrant community in Wisconsin, 1838-1918 (thesis). Cambridge, MA : Harvard University.

Long, B. (1983). In His vineyard 1868 to 1983. Pulaski, WI : Franciscan Publishers.

Lorimer, M. (2007). Ordinary Sisters: the story of the Sisters of St. Agnes 1858-1990. Fond du Lac, WI : Congregation of the Sisters of St. Agnes.

McCarthy, T. P. (1958). Guide to the Catholic Sisterhoods in the United States. Washington, D.C. : The Catholic University of America Press.

Naturalization Record of Rev. John Zawistowski 23 October 1863, Superior Court, Buffalo, NY vol. 261, no. 13705.

Obituary of Rev. Clement Rogożinski The Catholic Citizen. (Milwaukee, WI) 25 May 1901.

Obituary of Rev. Wiktor Zarecny, Dziennik Chicagoski (Chicago, IL), 9 November 1918.

Obituary of Rev. Louis Starostzick, Columbus Democrat (Columbus, WI), 5 September 1923.

Obituary of Rev. Joseph Chylewski, The Catholic Herald. (Milwaukee, WI) 7 April 1928.

Obituary of Rev. Sigmund Wożny, Oshosh Northwestern (Oshkosh, WI). 7 June 1937 p. 7.

Obituary of Msgr. Joseph C. Knitter, Herald Citizen (Milwaukee, WI), vol. 79, no. 38, 20 August 1949

Portrait and biographical album of Green Lake, Marquette and Waushara Counties, Wisconsin. (1890) Chicago, IL : Acme Publishing Co.

Princeton Republic, vol. V, no. 15, 20 May 1871.

Princeton Republic, vol. V, no. 41, 28 October 1871.

Princeton Republic, vol. XXI, no. 20, 2 June 1887

Princeton Republic, vol. XXI, no. 27, 27 july 1887.

Princeton Republic, vol. XXIII, 23 May 1889.

Princeton Republic, vol. XXX, no. 21, 14 June 1906.

Princeton Republic, vol. XXXVIII, no. 8, 26 February 1914.

Princeton Republic, vol. 64, 7 August 1930

Princeton Times Republic, 4 February 1932

Princeton Times Republic, vol. 70, 9 July 1936.

Princeton Times Republic, vol. 2, no. 9, 10 Septebmer 1936

Princeton Times Republic, vol. 76, 5 March 1942.

Princeton Times Republic, vol. 76, 12 March 1942.

Princeton Times Republic, vol. 76, 25 June 1942.

Princeton Times Republic, vol. 93, 8 October 1959.

Pula, J. (1995). Polish Americans : an ethnic community. New York : Twayne Publishers.

Sister Marie Elizabeth, C.J.C. (2011). Letter to author. Brockton, MA : Our Lady of Sorrows Convent.

Stevens Point Journal, 8 June 1988.

Sulimierski, F., Chebowski, B. & Walerski, W. (1902). Słownik geograficzny królestwa polskiego i innych krajów słowianskich. (CD version 2003) Chicago, IL : Polish Genealogical Society of America.

www.pgsny.org/Poland/priest_36.html

ACKNOWLEDGEMENTS

The Very Rev. Regis N. Barwig, Prior, The Community of Our Lady for his constant support of my projects.

Rev. Kenneth Augustine for the first tour of St. Albert's Cemetery, Milwaukee.

Duane F. Ebert for accompanying me on jaunts across Wisconsin to visit cemeteries and churches and correcting the manuscript.

Pat Born, Archivist, Diocese of Madison, Madison, WI.

Dariusz Smigielski, St. Adalbert's Cemetery, Niles, IL for his assistance in locating graves.

Fond du Lac Public Library, Fond du Lac, WI for getting me interlibrary loan materials.

John Okonek, Superintendent, Stevens Point Area Catholic Cemetery Association, Stevens Point, WI

Scott Mandernack, Head, Research & Instructional Services, Raynor Memorial Libraries, Marquette University, Milwaukee, WI.

Shelly Solberg, Archdiocesan Archivist and Eleanor Ryan, Archives Researcher, Archdiocese of Milwaukee Archives, Milwaukee, WI.

Sister Marie Elizabeth, C.J.C. for letter about Fr. Lopatto.

Columbus Public Library, Columbus, WI

Diane, Columbus Journal, (Capital Newspapers) Beaver Dam, WI

Susan Danna, St. Mary's Villa, Elmhurst Twp., PA for the photos of Rev. Lopatto's grave.

Denis Malchow for the visit to Holy Cross Cemetery and St. Albert's Cemetery, Milwaukee, WI.

Roger F. Krentz was raised in Princeton, WI and baptized in the Polish Catholic Parish Church of St. John the Baptist there. In the parochial school the School Sisters of St. Francis prepared him to received the Sacraments of Penance, First Holy Communion, and Confirmation. He has a B.A. from UW-Stevens Point, a MALS from UW-Milwaukee, and Ph.D. from UW-Madison. Krentz also studied at the Jagiełlonian University, Kraków, Poland. Dr. Krentz has taught on all levels from elementary school to university; has been a librarian on all levels from elementary school to university; has been an university administrator and a consultant. He divides his time between Wisconsin and New York.

Additional copies of this book may be purchased through: www.rogerfkrentz.com, www.Lulu.com, and www.amazon.com.

Other books by Roger F. Krentz, Ph.D.

Polish Catholic Churches in Wisconsin in 1905 according to Rev. Wacław Kruszka
The Bukowski Family of Green Lake & Marquette Counties, WI 1789-2009
The Czajkowski Family of Green Lake & Marquette Counties, WI 1794-2009
The Czarapata Family of Green Lake & Marquette Counties, WI & Cook County, IL 1816-2009
The Duszynski Family of Green Lake & Marquette Counties, WI 1770-2009
The Izban Family of Green Lake & Marquette Counties, WI 1756-2009
The Kranz Family of Green Lake & Marquette Counties, WI 1775-2009
The Marchel Family of Green Lake & Marquette Counties, WI & Cook County, IL 1807-2009
The Polus Family of Green Lake & Marquette Counties, WI 1771-2009
St. John the Baptist Catholic Church Princeton, WI: The 120th Anniversary of dedication 1888-4 November-2008 a testament of Polish immigrant faith

www.ingramcontent.com/pod-product-compliance
Lightning Source LLC
Chambersburg PA
CBHW041432300426
44117CB00001B/9